The Complete
Angel Wisdom
Workshop

The complete

Angel

Wisdom

Workshop

*Connect with your angels
bring love, healing and divine guidance
to every area of your life*

NATALIA COLMAN

Published in 2015 by Style Specialists
West Yorkshire, United Kingdom

Text © Natalia Colman 2015
Cover design: Randy V Tatad
Interior design: Soumi Goswami

A catalogue record for this book is available from the British Library.

ISBN 978-0-9570968-4-4

Printed and bound by CPI Group (UK) Ltd, Croydon, CR0 4YY

To Kelly,
Lots of love &
angel blessings
Natalie ♡

To my earth angels Estella, Tracy,
Andrew and Julie

*"How wonderful it must be
to speak the language of angels,
with no words for hate
and a million words for love!"*

CONTENTS

INTRODUCTION

Around 10 years ago, I worked as a fashion stylist, just like the style gurus in those TV shows 10 Years Younger, How to look Good Naked and What not to Wear. I would take people shopping, sort out their wardrobes and advise them about their style personality, body shape and what colours suited them best. After a while I realised that people would only come to see me at a certain point in their lives:

- *a significant age milestone; 30; 40; 50; 60*
- *a significant life event*
- *wanting to get promoted*
- *getting married*
- *the birth of their baby*
- *divorce/long-term relationship ending*
- *a bereavement.*

These life points also tend to coincide with becoming more aware of our life purpose and wanting to connect with our intuition. It's all about the inner work.

So what do I mean by that? Well, someone can tell you that you need to change your look, have a makeover, lose some weight, update your wardrobe, but the crisis point comes when you suddenly go inwards and your intuition tells you it's time to make a change.

These significant milestones in our lives often act as the catalyst but it can be other things as well. People who undergo huge weight loss talk about the defining moment when they suddenly noticed themselves in a photograph, got stuck in a seat on a plane, or overheard someone saying something nasty about their size.

This is true not just for making physical changes, it is also connected to those pivotal times when we need to change our life direction. It is only at the moment of enlightenment that we can make a shift and begin to make changes or ask for help; not before. Most of the time we trot through life, pushing aside what we sense is important and pretend it's not there, even though we know the truth.

Our inner voice speaks to us and we either don't want to listen, or it's not talking loudly enough for it to matter. So we just ignore it and carry on regardless. A little bit like the teacher in the Charlie Brown cartoons, all we hear is *"wah wah wah"*.

There comes a point in everyone's life when the inner voice speaks with such clarity and is shouting so loudly, that it cannot and will not be ignored. This is certainly what happened to me and I will share my own story with you. I tried to leave it out of the book but as you will discover, my angels would not let me!

The awakening and urgency of the inner voice is when something magical happens. We stop, we listen and we begin to process what we are hearing. The first message or moment of awakening can be traumatic. That's the initial encounter; like diving into cold water. After a little while the water begins to feel much nicer as we acclimatise to the temperature.

During these times that may seem like our darkest hours, our angels are there to help guide us. They aren't sinister or scary.

They are kind, wise, loving and caring; they want the very best for us. They want to help us accomplish everything we came here to do in this lifetime.

So have you reached a point at which you suddenly want to stop, listen and follow their advice and guidance? Are you ready to hear some important messages?

This book is all about helping you to tune your antenna better. You've done well tuning in so far and it's going to be a lifelong learning curve. So how can we benefit most from the presence of our angels? The most important thing you can do is to build a strong connection with your guardian angel; to ask for their guidance and tap into their wisdom.

This book will show you exactly how to build that connection, so that you can receive and channel messages from your angels. How will we do this?

I have divided the book into two parts. In part one I tell my story; how and why I came to be so interested in angels and how they have helped me change my life. I will show you practical ways in which you can build a closer connection with your own guardian angel. Part one also explores simple meditation techniques to allow you to find your calm centre and to improve your intuition. We will look at the many ways in which your angels will try to communicate with you and what this means. I will also introduce you to the three most powerful archangels and show you ways in which can connect with each of them for love, help, guidance and healing.

Part two of this book is devoted to the subject of angel cards. I will explain what angel cards are and how they differ to tarot cards, oracle cards and other forms of divination. Here I will show you how to interpret the messages within any deck of angel cards; how to prepare yourself and the space around you for a reading and how to structure an angel card reading for yourself and other people.

I will show you some of my favourite spreads to enable you to obtain guidance and messages from your angels, for readings relating to:

- *Love.*
- *Career/money.*
- *Health.*
- *Home and family.*
- *Life purpose.*
- *Spirituality.*
- *Direct questions with a yes or no answer.*
- *Daily angelic guidance.*
- *Timing of events and outcomes shown in a reading.*

Most importantly, the aim of this book is for me to pass on the important things I have learned. To enable you to open up a clear and continued connection with your angels. To bring important angelic answers and guidance into your life today.

Welcome to enlightenment through having the courage to listen to your inner voice. The good news for you is that life is just going to get better and better, your courage will be rewarded. You can turn the volume up on your inner voice and the connection with your angels. So pull up a chair and join me in the circle of inner truth; it's rather lovely in here.

PART I

DEVELOPING A CONNECTION
WITH YOUR ANGELS

*"Angels are all around us, all the time,
in the very air that we breathe"*

Eileen Elias Freeman

1

MY STORY

Lift the veil
Just a peek
A glimpse at you
Beneath the mask
You wear it so well…but it hides the truth

There once was a little girl called Natalia

19th July 2008 was the day that I moved out of my home. Just six weeks after my 40th birthday, I left my marriage of 17 years to begin a new life with my eight-year old daughter. At that time I was feeling a deep sense of disappointment with everything about my life. I felt in emotional pain and I knew I needed to move on and change my life. To find inner peace and true happiness.

Leaving my marriage was both the scariest and the bravest thing I have ever done. My husband is a good man. He is still a very dear friend and I will always feel blessed to have him in my life. However, the truth is that we just drifted apart over time and had become more like brother and sister. For around ten years before our marriage broke up I was feeling lost and unhappy. Why was this? Well I can probably pinpoint the root cause of where it all began; long before I ever met my husband. Let me take you back to when I was six years old.

Age six is when I first became aware that my parents were unhappy in their marriage and our home became like a battleground between them. Six more years of arguments, my father being constantly out of work and depressed and my mother having to support everyone financially and emotionally, created a very stressful home environment for me and my sister.

My mother is Mexican and when I was 12, she decided that she wanted to move back home to Mexico. This was a hugely traumatic upheaval for me because I thought I might never see England again.

I went straight to my new school in Mexico two weeks after we arrived. I couldn't speak Spanish; I was different to all the other kids and they hated me. I had to endure the most awful bullying. At best the kids completely ignored me; at worst they taunted me, played tricks on me, stole from my school bag and smashed eggs on my head. At break times I would run as fast as I could to the toilets before anyone saw me and hide in a cubicle. The eighteen months that I spent in Mexico were the unhappiest months of my life and would haunt me for many years to come.

During this period of time my Dad's depression reached a new low. He became unbearable to live with and the turf war between my parents turned explosive, often resulting in violent rages where he would go on the rampage, throw things and smash things up.

When we finally returned to the UK my parents broke up and divorced. My Dad's parting gift to us, before he left to go and live 200 miles away in London, was to rip up all our family photographs. After that I had no contact with him for a couple of years. He mellowed over time and managed to sort out his depression. Although we did eventually reconnect, our relationship was very strained.

The Chinese boyfriend

During that time of lacking a father figure in my life, I met a 31-year old man who was to become my first boyfriend.

I was fifteen years old when I met him. I had a Saturday evening job washing dishes in a Chinese restaurant and he was one of the restaurant owners. He was incredibly handsome, charismatic, had a lot of money and drove a fancy sports car. He looked more Italian than Chinese. Imagine a young Al Pacino or John Travolta and you are somewhere close. I was shocked when he began to take a great interest in me. He would spend hours chatting to me and always offered to drive me home after work. I developed a huge crush on him; he made me go weak at the knees. I couldn't believe that a man like this would ever be interested in me. The boys at school looked right through me as if I was invisible and whilst the other girls in my year had boyfriends, no one ever asked me out. I wasn't one of the popular girls. I was Natalia, the girl with the weird name. The girl with the foreign mother, the one who ate strange food, wore unfashionable clothes and didn't really fit in.

The week before my sixteenth birthday, during the car journey home from work, my Chinese man friend declared that he had very strong feelings for me. This was what I had dreamt of and couldn't believe my luck. He actually felt the same way about me! That night we kissed and it was wonderful, it was better than I ever imagined my first kiss would feel like. I fell head over heels in love right then and there.

He told me that his special birthday gift to me would be to take me shopping for a new dress. Then he would take me to lunch in a lovely hotel so I could wear my new outfit. So, on my sixteenth birthday, I had the amazing experience of being given the Pretty Woman treatment. Finally being treated like a grown up; being lavished with attention and going for a lunch that was fit for a princess.

As you are reading this you may have an inkling of what comes next. I didn't. I was quite a naïve sixteen-year old, so it had never occurred to me he had any motives other than being kind; but he had hatched an elaborate plan. To wine and dine me, then take me upstairs to the beautiful room he had booked for the rest of the afternoon. When he told me about the hotel room, all kinds of things were going through my mind. I didn't want to offend him, I felt obliged to him since he had been so generous towards me and I genuinely felt like I was in love with him. For the first time in my life I was with someone who made me feel so safe. What would happen if I said "No"? Would he leave me? I was petrified of losing him. So, I walked up the stairs to the hotel room that day and sealed another part of my fate. As I crossed the threshold of the room, I was about to close the door on my innocence and any shred of self-worth that I had left.

My relationship with my Chinese man-friend lasted nearly two years. It revolved around sex in return for taking me out to fancy places and buying me things. Every day after school he would be waiting at the gates in his sports car, ready to take me out for afternoon tea, to the cinema or shopping and then back to his house for sex. He wanted it every day and let's just say, he was very clear about exactly what he wanted from me. I got no pleasure from it and could not wait until it was over. He told me that women could not have an orgasm until they were in their thirties and stupidly I believed him.

You might think that the worst part of this was being used by this man, but it wasn't. The worst thing to me was that I had lied to my mother about sleeping with him. She wasn't happy about our relationship but this man was very predatory. She did try to tell me he wasn't good news, but I wouldn't hear a bad word said about him – I was addicted to him and he in turn, would not leave me alone.

By the time I was 17 and in the final year of studying for my A Levels, a stroke of luck happened. My Chinese man-friend announced he was going on a long holiday to Hong Kong to see his family and was planning to be away for three months.

The day he left I thought my heart would break in two. It really felt like he had died. Day after day I would cry myself to sleep. After a month of this utter grief, I had still not heard a word from him. It was as if he had disappeared off the face of the earth. He had telephoned the restaurant to let his partners know he was okay, but didn't bother to call me.

During the time he was away a strange thing happened. I began to see my life and my relationship with him with new eyes. It was like a bucket of cold water being thrown over me, but at the same time it gave me the enlightenment I would never have experienced had he still been around me every day. I slowly began to go out and meet people and make friends my own age. I started to do things that normal 17-year olds did. I went to nightclubs, went shopping with the girls and spent all my time with other teenagers having fun.

Life no longer revolved around being someone's sex object. I also discovered that I had blossomed into someone more attractive because suddenly other guys were starting to pay me attention and flirt with me. Something changed in that short time period and I was able to finally cut myself free of him. When he returned from his Hong Kong holiday, I told him our relationship was over.

Our relationship ended just as it began; with me sitting in the front seat of his car. After he listened to what I had to say, his parting words to me were these *"Well Natalia, you have a nice personality but you are fat and not very pretty. You'll be lucky to find someone else who fancies you"*. It was a cheap parting shot, but it hit the mark exactly where he wanted it to. I flung open the door and leapt out of his car, tears pouring down my face. I barely had a chance to slam the door shut before his car had screeched off into the night.

I left my job at the restaurant and shortly after, I moved 150 miles away to begin a college course. To this day I have never heard from him or seen him again. Out of sight out of mind? Definitely not; his words and actions would be tucked away in my memory and would continue to come back and haunt me.

My college years were much more fun and light hearted. There was a wonderful sense of freedom in being able to start again in a new place where no one knew me. I made a lot of new friends and life felt good for a while. That is until I began to date boys my own age. No matter what I did, every relationship I started to form ended in me being dumped from a great height. The boy I liked would be very keen for a while but would quickly lose interest in me. *"What on earth is wrong with me?"* I asked myself time and time again. No matter how hard I tried I couldn't seem to keep a relationship going for longer than three months. So my Chinese ex-boyfriend was right after all. Who would possibly want someone like me?

Married life

So now we will go forward in time to my next major life event; the point at which I met my husband. We met shortly before my 21st birthday. I had recently graduated from college and was in my first job. It paid very badly and I was renting a tiny flat in quite a poor neighbourhood of Bradford. I hated where I worked, I didn't know anyone in this city because all my friends from college had gone their separate ways. I was applying for jobs all over the country, but each time I was unsuccessful.

I stayed on in Bradford because my home town held too many dark memories. I definitely did not want to go back and live there again. My husband came into my life at a time when I was feeling lonely and vulnerable. He saw a value in me that no one else at the time could see (especially me). He opened up his heart and his home to me. For this I will be eternally grateful.

My soon-to-be husband was nine years older than me. He had done things I'd never experienced. He was calm, self-assured and seemed to know so much. Most importantly of all, he wanted me and he made me feel safe. I looked up to him and he seemed to adore being my teacher and mentor. Most importantly of all, he passed the big test of winning my mother's approval. She had never liked my first boyfriend (quite rightly so!) or any boyfriends that followed, but this time things were very different. He and my mum got along so well it was a pure delight to witness.

Within six weeks of meeting, we were living together very cosily in his house. We had even adopted our first kitten; Jerry. Life seemed perfect. Had I finally found the peace, love and security I had been looking for all my life?

The first home we shared together was the house he owned. It was quite small and we longed to have a place that was new to both of us. We found a beautiful character-filled cottage that had lots of space and overlooked open countryside. It was our dream home. We sold his house and moved into our cottage, getting engaged and married within a year of moving.

There were murmurings from my husband's family, who were quite surprised at how fast our relationship was progressing.

Although he was nearly thirty years old when we met, my husband had never lived with a girlfriend before and had never been in a relationship for longer than a year. His brother had strong words with him, telling him to slow things down, which was rather unnerving; but I will never forget the day that we moved into our first home together.

My husband was an excellent artist and was still firm friends with his art teacher from school; Mrs Cook. She and her husband came round to visit us and see the house. From the very beginning she was quite critical of me. She thought I was too young for him and voiced her opinions openly. As she walked around our new home and he proudly showed her all the rooms, she turned to him and said the words that would become etched in my memory: *"Make sure you get a contract to protect all of your things and exactly what YOU brought into this relationship financially. She has nothing and she deserves to take nothing of yours if you break up."*

Now, if you look at this logically, this was Mrs Cook's opinion and she was entitled to it. What she said was good advice, just delivered rather tactlessly. I have heard it said many times that everyone's actions have a positive intention. So Mrs Cook's positive intention was looking out for the best interests of her dear friend. However, her positive intention towards one person was having a very negative effect on me. Being the extremely sensitive young soul that I was at the time, her words wounded me to the very core. My eyes pricked with tears and a flash of anger welled up in me. *"How dare she say those things? Is that what everyone else is thinking and saying about me?"* I thought. Yet deep inside I knew her words had connected with the part of me that did not feel worthy of any of this. The man that loved me; the beautiful home. I was unlovable. Who did I think I was? I had no right to have any of this. I didn't deserve it. Everyone else knew this and she was simply confirming what I already knew myself, but did not want to admit to.

From that day the battle began. I was determined to prove that I was indeed worthy of everything I had. I would be the perfect wife. I would look after my man and my home impeccably. I would look perfect; that of course was very important. After all, my Chinese ex-boyfriend had pointed out that my value was attached to how I looked. In order to do this I needed to lose some weight, dress better and have perfect hair. I also needed to earn more money so that I could buy my way into the marriage. Yes, I was behind by a big deficit and I would have to make this up. I would bring in the money that I 'owed', prove my value in every way and silence the critics once and for all. So on that very day, the payback began.

My turbulent childhood and my relationship with my Chinese boyfriend was the precursor to this lack of self-worth. I did not feel like I was important, valuable or lovable. So I carried this with me into my marriage. It spilled over into my relationships with my family, my friendships and my work. Every day this lack of self-love was with me but buried deep inside. I was too afraid of my 'inner ugliness' to confront it. So I made the outside of me as beautiful as possible. The uglier and more unlovable I felt on the inside the harder I tried to create perfection on the outside and I got away with it for years. I fooled everyone, but I could never fool myself.

Let us fast forward in time again to the year of 2005. I had achieved every single thing that I set out to do. I was now very 'successful'. I spent years going to night school and getting qualifications. I climbed the corporate ladder, gained promotion after promotion. I then set up my own business straight after my daughter was born. I drove an expensive sports car and I worked all over the world as a business consultant getting paid up to £1000 per day. I flew business class to glamorous locations and stayed in fabulous hotels. I wore a gold Cartier watch, had wardrobes full of clothes, shoes and designer handbags. I lived in a detached house with a big garden and drank champagne in my hot tub. Life was beautiful, but only on the outside.

To the casual observer who glanced at a snapshot of my life, I had it all. My life was filled with luxurious 'stuff' but the more stuff I acquired the emptier I felt. I worked hard, very hard. I worked so hard that a typical day would consist of getting up at 5am so I could afford the time to take my daughter to school. I always worked in the evening until 10 or 11pm. Sometimes when I had a very tight deadline or a huge workload, I would work right through the night to get it all done. I constantly worked at weekends and rarely had a day off.

I was away so often travelling that I didn't get to see a lot of my daughter and the guilt of this was eating away at me. If you're a parent then you will understand how this feels. Your children seem to always have some kind of crisis, large or small that inconveniently happens when you are away. So much military precision goes into organising everything when you want to take some time away from your kids, and the very fact that you are not there with them does tug on your heartstrings.

I got to breaking point during this period where I could take the pressure no longer. I wanted to be free of this burden of having to be perfect and having to pay back what I owed to be in the marriage. I decided that I had done enough and now would be my time. It was time for me to do what I had always wanted to do. My drive to succeed was now being replaced with resentment.

Over the years I felt as though Natalia had got lost. Who was I? Why did I still feel so worthless even though I seemed to have everything? I felt as though I had no peace in my life. The solution to this really felt like it was about doing what I had always wanted to do. When I was a child I was very creative and I loved to write. There was this very strong pull making me want to uncover those childhood dreams. Surely enough was enough. I had well and truly proved myself and I had suffered enough.

The metamorphosis begins

Kaleidoscope wings

Gossamer thin

Your delicate beauty hides

Your struggle to become

The butterfly you are within

So, rather tentatively I sat down with my husband and broached the subject of changing my career. I had always loved clothes and fashion and I wanted to retrain to become a fashion stylist. I had grand plans in my mind about using some of my hard-earned money to go on a fashion styling course in New York. Then I would set up a practice back home, taking people shopping, helping them sort out their wardrobes. I also dreamt about writing a book about all of this to help people.

The response I got was far worse than I was expecting. He was so shocked and so against the idea, the whole conversation blew up into a bitter argument. I now realise it was all about fear. His fear that I was taking away the security blanket I'd given him for years, of earning lots of money and giving us our fabulous lifestyle. He had gotten so accustomed to it, he didn't want anything to jeopardise this. My fear was based around not being able to spend time with my daughter and being locked in a cycle of working on things that I really did not care about. I felt trapped and I wanted to be free to explore my true passion in life.

After much grumbling my husband finally agreed to my plans and I went off to New York to do my training. The problem was that he never really bought into my plan. He thought what I was doing was worthless (see that word is coming up again). The cracks in our marriage started to spread and deepen.

I loved my new work with a passion I hadn't felt in years. However, I only succeeded in bringing in a fraction of what I had been earning and this caused more and more problems. My husband nagged me to go back to my business consulting work. I began to feel as though my only value was as a cash cow that kept the luxurious lifestyle afloat and provided financial security; as though none of my needs were considered important.

In truth, what I couldn't see was that I had created this situation. My lack of self worth had given me the identity of provider. When I decided that I didn't want to do it any more, I had effectively pulled the rug from under my husband's feet. I had created a monster within my marriage. I was responsible for all of it but I blamed him. I felt so unhappy that the only relief from this was to go shopping. Buying shoes and clothes gave me a nice little high; it also gave me approval from other people. They would look at me as if I was still affluent and successful. I know now, this is temporary and all the 'stuff' in the world will never fill a gaping void in one's life.

The lost years

So, in 2008 we finally realised that our marriage was unsalvageable and took the joint decision to divorce. My husband wanted to stay in the house; something I was quite relieved about. I wanted a fresh start. I had never truly been on my own and never independently owned my own home. I felt I was ready to experience this even though it had come a little late in life. I moved out with my daughter into a rented house until I could find a home to buy.

No matter how much you want change, it will never happen fully unless you have the courage to embrace it. Within a week of moving into my rented house I felt so scared and alone, it nearly drove me to edge of reason. I felt like I just couldn't cope emotionally without a man by my side. After all, I had been in a relationship since the age of 16. It didn't matter that my first relationship made me feel worthless or that I singlehandedly carried the second relationship. I couldn't face the thought of being on my own. So within two weeks of leaving my husband, I plunged head first into a four-year relationship with a man who I will call Daniel.

The first six months of the relationship were perfectly fine, but the months and years that followed were like sheer torture. We were so incompatible but we could not find a way of breaking off the relationship. It was as though there was an invisible cord connecting us. The entire relationship was based around fear. He was afraid of commitment and spent the whole four years running away from me. When Daniel ran away I would sometimes run after him. Other times I would retreat in despair that he didn't want me. He would then come pinging back as though he was attached to a piece of elastic. He said and did some very cruel things, but I made allowances for this because I was afraid of being alone. That is why I would chase him and why I took him back over and over again. Far from having the peace of mind I craved, I was now a nervous wreck.

To this day I really do not know what I saw in Daniel. When we met he told me he was taking a 'career break'. What that basically meant was he had no job. He was 45 years old and living with his parents after his own marriage had broken down. He also had a myriad of his own insecurities and a troubled childhood to go along with these. His life was littered with broken marriages, a child he abandoned years ago as a baby and had severed all contact with and a fifteen-year old son who lived hundreds of miles away and had begun to rebel and reject him as a father.

We were two troubled people and our relationship spelt disaster. Daniel's way of dealing with his troubles was to lash out at me.

He would project all his insecurities onto me and strip away my confidence little by little. He would be calm and happy one minute and the next he would flip into a violent, jealous rage. Unfortunately he wasn't discerning about when this happened. He would start shouting at me in the middle of the street, during dinner in a restaurant and even in a middle of watching a film at the cinema – that one was the most embarrassing of all. A good-looking actor appeared on the screen and Daniel looked across at me to see my expression. I smiled at him and laughed and then suddenly he flew into a wild temper, accusing me of fancying this actor who was a lot younger than me. All the way home he told me I was perverted and nothing better than a paedophile.

I cried every day during the final year of our relationship and towards the end, I very wisely kept him well away from my daughter.

Our relationship ended in a huge, explosive argument. It had to end that way. Daniel tried to kick my front door in, ransacked my home and said things to me that I won't ever repeat. I recorded his rantings on my mobile phone just in case I needed them as evidence. Thankfully, after two hours of this torment, I managed to get him to leave and as soon as he had gone I called the police. They were so kind and helpful, which in a way made me feel worse for having to bring them into this situation. They arranged to have the locks on my front door changed immediately. Mercifully, my daughter was way on holiday with her Dad at the time, so she never witnessed any of this.

That was the final straw, it took this episode for me to really see the light and I was finally able to walk away. It also had the same effect on Daniel and although I feared he might come back, he never did. He carried out a few vindictive acts from a distance, such as having my internet disconnected and sending me threatening emails asking for money he said I owed him. He had said and done far worse things in the past, by this time I was numb to it all.

For the first time in my life I finally realised that I did not love and value myself and that if I did not press pause on my relationships, I would attract the same things into my life over and over again. I would lurch from being in a relationship, experiencing great frustration and anguish, then breaking it off, finding myself single, lonely and emotionally destroyed.

I realised now that meeting Daniel was a gift from the Universe. You may wonder why I would say this. Well, this is because if I had met someone relatively level headed, I would have carried on feeling inadequate and worthless deep down. My insecurities and troubles would have bubbled up sooner or later in a relationship with a functional person. They would have continued to run rampage through my life until I brought them to the surface and dealt with them. I was the one that had to change. So I decided not to embark on any romantic relationships until I had done this.

On each birthday, for as many years as I can remember, I felt sad, empty and fearful about getting older. My life felt incomplete and whilst I experienced snatched moments of happiness, beneath the surface I was deeply discontent. It was during my darkest time of truly being alone that I knew I simply could not do this any more, be this person, live this life, and feel this way. To outward appearances I was smiling confident and successful Natalia. I had pulled this off many times and so the lie continued.

In that moment I decided to change my life. It was a journey I could not put off any longer. The call had been there many times, but this was the first time I'd really listened to it. This time I felt ready and brave enough to step forward and answer it.

I knew this would be the biggest challenge I had ever faced, to make lasting changes, to create a life for myself that I loved by healing my past and facing up to who I was; my true authentic self. Would I be able to do it? I wanted this with every fibre of my being and I knew that this moment of recognition and honesty was going to be the biggest and most important step towards my brand new life.

Must be talking to an angel

Be calm

Be still

Take gentle breaths

And fall in love

With life again

I have to admit that this going 'cold turkey' with relationships and being completely on my own was terrifying. So
terrifying in fact, that I would lie awake for hours on end
every night, in floods of tears and feeling a complete sense
of hopelessness. Who was I if I didn't have someone to love
me and hold my hand? I had no one I could confide in about
this because I felt so ashamed and stupid about all of the
mistakes I had made in my life. I also did not want to tell
anyone the truth about how I was feeling. Yes I was ready to
face up to having reached rock bottom, but I was still putting
on a brave face to the outside world. I couldn't bear anyone
knowing the truth, so I kept everything to myself and carried on pretending.

I had felt worthless many times in my life before this, but usually
I pushed it back into the darkness, pretended it didn't exist and
just bought more clothes or worked harder to distract myself. I
knew I couldn't do that any more. The lid was now completely
off the jar and everything that I had been covering up was right
there in front of me. I look back now and I see what a brave
thing I did but also how incredibly scary it was. As I write this
I have so much compassion for myself, but I didn't have any at
that time. I beat myself up terribly, punished myself for having
done such stupid things. I told myself I'd ruined my life and this
made me feel even worse.

Three years earlier, I had moved to a new town where I knew no one, so the only people I had in my life at the time were Daniel and my daughter. My mother lived 100 miles away and was devastated about my marriage breakup. She disliked Daniel intensely; she was very angry with me and so, my relationship with her had broken down quite badly at that time. "*I deserve all of this*" I told myself.

I have always loved angels and collected angel statues and ornaments. It was during one of these moments of utter grief, when I felt that life wasn't worth living that I asked for help from my angels. I started by speaking out loud to them. I had a little angel ornament in a pebble of clear resin that sat on my bedside table. It was called an 'Angel Worry Stone'. I held this angel stone tightly in my hand as I spoke to my angels asking for help. I would do this every night and quite often I would feel this wave of calmness sweep over me, the tears would stop and I was able to go to sleep. Night after night, I held the angel in my hand and began to speak to my angels. I imagined what they would look like. I imagined them as smiling, beautiful, kind and loving.

This became a ritual for me and turned into something I really looked forward to doing. I would go off to sleep holding the angel stone and talking to them. If I woke up in the middle of the night, my conversations with my angels would begin again until I fell asleep. The conversations I had with them (I call these conversations because it really did feel as though 'someone' was listening to me) mostly consisted of me telling my angels how I felt; sharing my problems with them and asking for help. There was something so comforting about doing this. It felt crazy in a lot of ways, but at the same time I didn't care. It made me feel better, more peaceful and I actually felt as though someone was listening to me.

I had a conversation recently with a lady who had a very bad cancer experience; one where she was literally at death's door. She told me that she would hold a crystal in her hand during the time when she was in hospital and at the point of the gravest stage of her illness. We talked about how it was so comforting to hold something in your hand. I have since discovered that there is a chakra (an energy centre) in each palm of the hand. These particular chakras are powerful tools of perception and healing.

After a while, little things started to happen. I felt as though I was being given signs from my angels; I began to notice the signs and I took action. This happened because I had opened up the channels of communication with my angels. I had somehow tuned into their frequency and once I had done it, the flood gates opened and they seemed to communicate with me every day. I was being guided through my intuition to go to certain places, pick up the phone and talk to certain people. Ideas popped into my head, seemingly from nowhere, and I followed up on them. I put my trust and faith in the angels' wisdom and I followed through.

My conversations with the angels continued and I experienced many miracles in my life and my work, both great and small. There are too many to list here, but I will share a few of my favourite ones with you throughout the book. It was the small miracles that had the biggest impact on me. They were like little affirmations from my angels. Calling cards that meant so much. I thought of it as their way of showing me that they cared; their reminder to me that I was never alone and I was always being loved and cared for.

My chats with my angels evolved over time. They started out as anguish-filled counselling sessions and grew into cosy chats, where I shared my thoughts about the day. I expressed my gratitude about how my life was unfolding and changing into something more meaningful. It was also an opportunity to say thank you and I love you. In doing this I also began to love and accept myself more and more; to believe I was worthy of love and all the good things that were happening to me. This time, the things that were happening weren't about filling a void, they were about being mindful. About seeing everything that was good in my world and enabling me to realise that I had everything I needed. It was simply a case of adjusting my vision and seeing everything anew.

One of the biggest lessons I learned during this time was about being alone. I had always hated it and tried to avoid it as much as possible. It was during the alone times when I got the greatest flashes of insight and wisdom. This has continued to be the case ever since. Now I embrace and look forward to chunks of time when I am going to be alone; I realise that these will bring me my greatest rewards.

And so my development continued. I went along to spiritual talks and events. I began to be brave enough to openly speak up in front of a group people and tell the truth about how I felt and share some of my darker life experiences. The interesting thing is that no one judged me; or maybe I was so past caring that I didn't notice whether they were or not. The most important thing became telling the truth.

Over the four years with Daniel I had gained 50 pounds through drinking wine every evening to drown my sorrows and through comfort eating. I went up three dress sizes, I began to experience pain in my knees and I felt so unattractive. I asked my angels for help me with my weight loss and to help me to eat more healthily. A few days later I was driving to pick my daughter up from a sports event she was doing. I had to drive to a part of town I had never been before and suddenly I saw a sign for a gym. The gym had a big banner across its front gates advertising a weight loss programme. I pulled over to the side of the road and went straight into the gym. The lady who ran the weight loss programme was a beautiful and very friendly young woman called Rachel. She was so helpful and before I knew it I had signed up to a six-week programme with her. The best thing about it was that it involved being given recipes and lists of fabulous, healthy food to eat, an exercise plan and it also involved giving up alcohol and coffee for the six week period.

I embraced this health and fitness programme wholeheart-edly. I loved it so much and found Rachel so supportive that I signed up for a further six weeks. I lost every single one of those 50 pounds and Rachel became a close friend. It was as if my angels had presented me with the solution to my weight problems and a new friend all in one.

My turbulent childhood was the time when my confidence and self worth took a battering. For a long time I blamed my parents and was very resentful for what I felt they had put me through. Now I realise that they are only human, they were doing the best that they could. They both had difficult upbringings too, so the pattern had continued. My mother bravely supported us all for years, singlehandedly raising us and providing for us. She never complained, she just got on with it and looking back, I see she did a magnificent job and is an inspiration to me now as a mother myself.

In the seventies and eighties when I was growing up, not a lot was known about mental health and depression. Looking back, I am convinced that my Dad was suffering from bipolar or some other form of mental health problem. He did not get the help he needed and his struggles resulted in violent mood swings and quite often extreme and abusive behaviour. I now know that he wasn't to blame, if he had been given the right support and medication, perhaps things would have been a whole lot different. He wasn't a great father to me, but he has a strong bond as grandfather to my daughter. They get along very well and love one another very much.

The most important and positive thing about all of this is I know that both my parents did and still do, really love me and want the best for me. They were struggling to deal with their lives in the only way they could find at the time. It was during this time when I was building my connection to my angels, that I got the message that I needed to forgive my parents, my first boyfriend, my husband, Daniel. Most of all I needed to forgive myself.

Each and every one of us had experienced things that made us behave in a certain way. We were all incomplete in some way; all acting through fear. None of us were to blame and it was in this moment of clarity that I was able to look at the situation and see it for what it truly was. I realised that all my 'mistakes' were learning experiences. The choices that I made that weren't for my highest good, taught me so many things and led me to this calm space. The suffering put me on the path to enlightenment.

Angel Lady is Born

"A funny thing happens when we stand up taller than we dared…the whole Universe lines up and the divine orchestra plays a symphony so damn beautiful, it blows your eardrums down into your heart and they beat together in unison, and you hear yourself louder than ever before…if you dare. I dare. I always choose to dare"

Erin Faith Allen

It was from this more powerful place that I decided I needed to give something back to my angels. I wanted to honour them by finding out much more about how this all worked. So I began to buy books, do research on the internet and learn as much as I possibly could about angels. I went from a place of neediness and desperation to one of gentle power; to a place of honesty and recognition of who I was at a soul level. Nothing from my past could hurt me any more. I had faced up to the fear and the thought of facing the fear was far scarier than anything the fear had to offer, so it seemed to just melt away.

The answer was simple to me now. I had discovered my angels and the angelic wisdom inside myself. I had developed a connection that was now a constant source of positivity. I was able to sense the right thing to do and say in almost every situation. Most of all, I had love and compassion for myself and everyone around me. This changed every single relationship I had, from my day-to-day interactions with my daughter and my mother, through to rekindling relationships with friends I'd lost touch with and the customers who I worked with. I made the most of this angelic bond I seemed to have developed and I was on a mission to find out more and get even closer.

It was then that I began to research everything I could about angels. I read books; I scoured the internet and I bought some angel cards, although I had no idea how to read them. I kept seeing repeating numbers on the clock on my phone and bedside alarm clock and I wondered what this meant. I remembered reading somewhere that repeating numbers were like a form of 'angel Morse code' so I decided to look up the meaning on the internet. I found Doreen Virtue's website which explained the different numbers and their meanings. As I was trying to select a certain web page to look at a specific number meaning I clicked on a different link by mistake and this brought up the details of the Doreen Virtue's Angel Practitioner workshop in London. As I looked through the details I discovered that this was to be Doreen's last ever London workshop. I knew in that moment this was a sign and I needed to book myself a place.

Off I went to London and spent the most wonderful time learning all about angel meditation, connecting on an even deeper level with my angels and how to read angel cards. Attending this was like opening up a portal in my mind. I suddenly found I had unlocked something; I could look at the angel cards and see real meaning in them. This felt like the missing piece of the jigsaw.

When I came back from London, I felt strongly that I wanted to help other people. It felt like everywhere I went, people were lost and unhappy, just like I had been. They seemed to be searching for meaning and not knowing how or where to find it. I just didn't know exactly what it was I should do. Several months went by and I waited for some direction from my angels.

One day over the Christmas holidays I was alone at home and my daughter was with her Dad. I was feeling a little sorry for myself, being alone at this time of year when everyone else was with their families. My iPad was sitting open on the kitchen table and a familiar wave of intuition came over me. My intuition said *"set up a Facebook page and call it Angel Lady"*. So that is what I did; right then and there. I sent an invitation to my Facebook friends to 'Like' the page and as I did this I was suddenly gripped with fear. *"What if people think I'm completely out of my mind?" I thought to myself.* Luckily my higher self was quick to jump in. It responded with *"You are doing this with a positive intention. You are trying to help people; people will always think and say things about you, that's none of your business. Your business is helping people who need it most".* So that is what I did, I pushed aside my fear and concentrated on taking my first steps; creating this 'Angel Lady' page.

The response has been fantastic and I had no need to worry. Most days I write an uplifting message. I select angel cards for people, record guided meditations and generally it is a place where we can discuss all things angelic. What I did not realise is just how many people are interested in and believe in angels. However, it all seems to be undercover. We often don't discuss our beliefs about angels, but so many people love them and are inspired by them.

From the day I began my Angel Lady page, I have let my intuition and my angels guide me about what to put there and what to do with it. One day I had an overwhelming flash of inspiration, to create a workshop called 'Angel Wisdom'. So many of my Facebook followers are scattered all over the UK and indeed, all over the world. Hence, I have been guided to create a workshop that people can learn from through extensive written notes and videos. As I was writing the notes for this distance learning workshop I found that I couldn't just type out the key information. I was writing and writing and writing and I couldn't stop. Every time I tried to stop and keep the notes simple, I found myself typing at great speed and the words just flowed. It was then that I realised my angels wanted me to write this book. Once I began I could not stop.

As I write, I kept getting the same words coming up in my mind over and over again *"Tell the truth"*. That is why I began this book by telling you my story.

2

WHO AND WHAT ARE ANGELS?

"Angels have no philosophy but love"

Terri Guillemets

Jimi Hendrix, Madonna, Fleetwood Mac and Robbie Williams amongst many others have all written songs about them. In our lifetime, the idea of angels seems to have become a much wider part of popular culture, but Angels have always been a part of civilization. The notion of their existence, passed down through stories, ancient texts, songs or word-of-mouth.

Although we talk about angels and we might believe in them, who are they and what do they do? There are many well-known 'angel gurus' and some of my favourite angel intuitives and teachers include Doreen Virtue, Radleigh Valentine, Diana Cooper, Kyle Gray, Lorna Byrne and Chrissie Astell. All of them have written about their personal encounters and beliefs about angels. Whilst their thoughts and descriptions of angels vary somewhat, they all agree on one thing; angels are beautiful light beings of pure love. Their sole mission and purpose is to serve, guide and protect us.

From what I have researched and read about angels, there are many different theories. Some thought leaders, such as Doreen

Virtue, believe that we have two angels with us in this lifetime, one to comfort us and the other to nudge us to stay on the right path and fulfil our life's purpose. Others believe that we have a single guardian angel, but other angels can be drafted in to help us during the most critical and testing periods of our lives.

One thing I do feel is that we have at least one guardian angel who is assigned to us individually. It is my belief that we sit down and discuss this life with our guardian angel before we are born into this particular lifetime. We agree with our guardian angel what we will set out to do and learn in this lifetime. Who our parents will be, who we will meet, befriend, marry, love, parent, become friends and enemies with and what our purpose and lessons will be. Our astrological birth chart fits all of this perfectly.

Of course, we forget all of this as soon as we are born and during our life we have to figure it out as we go along. At a soul level, we are still conscious of our life lessons and what our purpose is. When we truly go inwards, that is when we can connect with some of the answers. Our guardian angel accompanies us along each step of the way, protecting and guiding us and giving us complete and utter unconditional love.

Now when you read this about having a life purpose and a certain destiny it might be tempting to say: *"Okay, well seeing as all of this is going to happen anyway I might as well just sit back and let it happen since I have no influence on events that will occur in my life."* The opposite is true. You have a great force of will over your life. Yes, there is a certain lesson that you need to learn in this lifetime and certain skills and talents you have been given to help, like tools of the trade. You are also destined to meet certain other people in this life and there will be tests you will be put through. However, the success you make of it is entirely up to you.

Sometimes we achieve outstanding things in this life, other times we just get in under the wire or we simply don't do the necessary work or learn the lessons. We have a lot of work to do over many lifetimes so you can accomplish a whole heap of things in this life, do the bare minimum or do nothing at all. One thing is for sure, you will keep going through lifetimes until you have learned what you need to learn and done what you need to do. The choice is yours and your life really is in your hands.

What is widely written is that our angels cannot intervene or interfere in our lives unless we ask them for their help. There is one exception to this and that is if we are in grave danger and risk dying before our time. In which case they can protect us and there have been many stories told of this very thing happening.

This is powerful stuff! Whether you believe in all this or not, to me it is a very comforting thought to know that there is a loving presence with us at all times. A guiding light that is rooting for us when we experience our greatest achievements and comforting us during our darkest times.

So if these faithful guardians are here solely to support us without interfering, how can we benefit from their presence? The most important thing you can do is to build a strong connection with your guardian angel, to ask for their guidance and to learn to tune in to their loving messages and tap into their wisdom.

There is a saying that you shouldn't worry about how you'll do something, your angels and the Universe will take care of that. All you have to do is know what you want and keep showing up and taking action; put one foot in front of the other.

There are a few questions that I'd like you to consider. These are BIG questions, so I don't expect you to have the answers to them right now. But I would like you to mull them over.

Write a few notes down alongside those questions that you feel an instant response to.

What about the other questions that you cannot answer right now? Just sit with those and come back to them. Take your time. The answers will unfold; I can assure you of that because your angels will help you to answer each and every one of them.

What do I want my life to be like?

Who am I being right now?

What am I afraid of?

What is making me unhappy?

What am I putting up with in my life?

What do I need to let go of?

What have I always wanted to do?

Who can help me?

How do I want to feel?

What do I need to heal?

3

PRACTICAL WAYS TO BUILD AN ANGELIC CONNECTION

"I saw the angel in the marble and carved until
I set him free."

Michelangelo

So, why build a connection with your guardian angel(s)?

Connecting to our angels doesn't stop bad things from happening to us. It helps us choose love as the best option every time. It helps us move away from fear and recover quicker from painful experiences.

Angels can't save you from difficult situations but they will help you recognise the strength that is within you. They will take you to somewhere that you can find comfort and healing. Our angels push us to find solutions – they are the unseen force, the inner voice that tells you what to do and where to go next.

I talked earlier about angels being pure love and light. We're going to do an exercise that I first learned from attending a workshop with Angel Intuitive, Kyle Gray. This will to help enlighten you a little more about your own guardian angel.

- Sit comfortably, relax and close your eyes.

- Now I'd like you to imagine someone whom you love very deeply. This can be a person alive or in spirit or even a beloved pet. Think about how this person or animal makes you feel.
- Imagine their face, radiant and happy.
- Think what it is about them that is so lovable.
- Really step into and embrace those feelings that you get when you are with them and you think of them.
- Just bask in the warm glow of knowing how much you love them and how good it feels to be with them.
- Now bring your awareness back to being in the room and slowly open your eyes.
- How did that feel? I have done this exercise many times myself and with others and people say it makes them feel warm, comforted, serene, peaceful and filled with total joy.

I asked you to do this because I wanted to give you a glimpse of how your guardian angel feels about you – isn't that wonderful?

Your guardian angel's only purpose is to serve you, to guide and protect you throughout your lifetimes.

Your guardian angel is here for you and you alone – no one else knows you better than they do or loves you more than they do. They already have a powerful connection to you and there are certain things you can do to tune in to them and receive their guidance more clearly.

Guardian Angel Meditation

Meditating takes you from your thinking state to a higher state of consciousness; allowing you to connect with your feeling energy rather than your thoughts. The mind operates from a place of fear which is the ego. This keeps us safe and alive and is trying to rationalise all the time. Connecting with our senses and feelings during meditation takes us to a different state, one that allows the connection to really flow.

Many people tell me that they don't like to meditate because they can't do it or they feel fidgety and cannot stop thinking about other things. Meditation takes a little practice and is a bit like doing exercise. It can feel a little strange and uncomfortable at the beginning, but after a while we build 'muscles' and we begin to really enjoy it. When we enjoy something we want to do it more because it gives us a sense of well-being. There are many studies that have been done that prove the benefits of meditation. You don't have to spend hours on end meditating it's not a competition. To really feel the benefits and to build, strengthen and maintain the connection to your angels you need to meditate often. I recommend meditating every day for at least five minutes. No matter how busy we are, we can all set aside five minutes in the course of our day to sit peacefully and meditate. You will be glad you began this and once you begin you will look forward to doing it – I can assure you of that.

A guided meditation to meet your guardian angel

Find a comfortable position either sitting or lying down. Make sure you are warm enough or cool enough and that you will not be disturbed for the next five minutes.

When you are settled and ready, relax and rest your hands on your lap or on the tops of your legs, with your palms facing upwards.

Close your eyes and let your thoughts drift away. Just con-centrate on your breathing. Take a deep breath in through

---

your nose, inflating your belly and taking the breath all the way down to the base of your spine. Now breathe out and as you exhale, imagine all your cares and worries floating away with the breath.

Imagine there are roots growing out of the soles of your feet, going deep into the ground, making you at one with the earth and keeping you safe and secure.

Now imagine there is a bright white light above your head. Imagine that the light begins to shower down around you like a waterfall. It feels beautiful and warm, safe, soothing and healing as it cascades and begins to surround your body.

Imagine the light growing and surrounding you like a huge bubble of energy, the light is now three feet wide and surrounds every part of your body, sealing and protecting you.

Now imagine the chakra on the top of your head is like a lotus flower that is closed tightly. Imagine this lotus flower at the top of your head opening up and as it opens and all of the petals unfold the white light begins to flow through your body filling up your head and your face. Imagine the light travelling down through your throat and shoulders, down through your chest, along your arms down to your wrists and fingers.

The white light flows along your stomach, your hips and down along your legs, through your knees to your calves, ankles and through your feet and out to your toes.

All of your body is now radiant and receiving the beautiful love and healing energy of this white light.

Now I'm going to ask your guardian angel to gently step forward - your angel has their arms outstretched and they are so filled with joy to connect with you. Your angel gently takes your hands and enfolds you completely in their wings, enveloping you with love and protection

Take a few moments to enjoy the bliss of being with your guardian angel be aware of any sensations. If you would like to ask them a question then you can do this in your mind. What is your guardian angel's name? You can ask your angel anything you like, just take a few moments to be with them; listen and feel their presence

Your guardian angel is now going to gently unfold their wings and let go of your hands. They have a gift for you and it is a huge diamond that is the size of the palm of your hand. Your angel would like you to imagine the chakra inside your heart opening up like a flower your angel is going to place the huge glittering diamond inside the space within your heart chakra. The rainbow colours from the diamond are now showering out of your heart chakra, illuminating the entire room with its beauty. Your angel would now like you to close your heart chakra by imagining it closing up like the petals of a flower. The beautiful diamond of love that your angel has given you is now sealed within your heart space so that you can carry the love of your guardian angel in your heart forever.

Your angel showers you one last time with white light and their blessings and they will remain with you guiding, healing and supporting you. Your angel disappears in a shower of stars into the background but leaves their loving energy with you.

Now I would like you to begin to sense being back in the room, gently and slowly begin to move your fingers, wiggle your toes and when you are ready, open your eyes.

You may wish to make some notes about this meditation so that you can look back over them in the future.

How did that meditation feel?

What did you sense?

What did you see?

What did you hear?

What did you feel?

Was your angel male, female or genderless?

Did they give you their name?

This meditation is a wonderful way of building the connection with your guardian angel. You can do it time and time again. You will sense, see, hear and feel different things every time that you do it. Sometimes the meditation will be rich with messages, images and sensations. Other times you may not pick up on much at all. But no meditation time is ever wasted. Simply sitting in a state of complete relaxation, switching off from the chatter of your mind, your cares and worries and connecting with your higher self is all wonderfully healing and will improve your well-being.

In the future you can do this meditation and sit with your angel to ask them specific questions and for guidance about certain areas of your life. Other times you may wish to connect with them for comfort if you are feeling unhappy or for healing if you are feeling unwell. You may wish to tell them something or to thank them or just simply to feel closer to them.

There is no right or wrong way to do this meditation. If you fall asleep during the meditation, you have not missed out. You might not be able to consciously recall messages or sensations from connecting with your angel, but you will have benefitted at an unconscious level. It also means that you have reached a deep state of relaxation; so congratulations.

Subsequent times when you do this meditation you can ask your angel in your mind to give you another gift instead of a diamond. Take notice of what they give to you. You can look up the symbolic meaning of the gift by searching for this on the internet. You can type into an internet search engine:

Spiritual meaning of a.... then add in the blank space whatever the gift was that your angel gave you. This is a very interesting thing to do. I have been given many things by my guardian angel during meditations, including a violin; the letter M and even a frog!

Letters and numbers have significance too. Letters have a meaning in numerology so you can look these up. All of these things may seem unusual to you but that is how your angels will begin to connect and send you messages. The stronger the connection you build, the more that you will begin to understand a common language and you will begin to sense and interpret exactly what your angel is trying to tell you and how they are trying to guide you. Over time, you will find that the connection is so strong, you will be able to channel their messages during everyday life. This is certainly what I have found and it is a truly powerful and very wonderful thing. So just sit back and enjoy the process.

Creating an Angel Journal

Each one of the interactions we have with our angels is important in its own way. I will be honest and say that quite often, the messages you will receive may not make any sense to you at the time.

At the beginning, while you are building the relationship, it can be a little bit like collecting the pieces of a puzzle. The signs and symbols may be baffling and you cannot see the bigger picture until you have collected quite a few of them. For this reason, I can highly recommend keeping an angel journal.

An angel journal is a personal notebook that is devoted to recording any images, feelings, thoughts and messages that come into your mind before, during and after your conversations, meditations and requests to your angels. The most important thing about keeping a journal is that you must do it in the way that best suits you.

Some people prefer to keep all their notes in one place; others prefer to have different journals or notebooks for different purposes. It may be that you are more comfortable with technology than you are with paper. You might find that typing up any thoughts and messages into the notes section of your mobile phone, tablet or laptop works better for you.

My mobile phone is often the closest thing to hand, so any thoughts or messages that come to be during a meditation or in a dream can be recorded very quickly on there before I forget about them.

I do love keeping journals and have a range of pretty books that I transfer my notes into later on. This enables me to keep a more permanent record of messages and guidance. I look back over these journals and I find that the things I wrote about a few months or years ago begin to make more sense to me. I can also see patterns emerging. For example, when I first began to do the meditation to connect to my guardian angel I found that I felt a sense of lightness and happiness but I didn't see anything. I found it quite difficult to imagine what my angel looked like. Over time, I found that my angel began to emerge and look like a person. She was female, a beautiful lady with long, brown, wavy hair. Every time I did the meditation I would keep a record of the images I saw and what sensations came over me. During one meditation my angel gave me a violin as a gift. I wasn't sure what this meant, but I made a note of it.

During each meditation, the same beautiful lady would appear and I kept on asking this angel what her name was. After several more meditations the name 'Cecilia' popped into my mind. I wrote this name down in my journal. A few weeks later, I was visiting my mother for the weekend and I mentioned to her that I'd been meditating with my guardian angel and that I finally had received a name from her. My mother asked me what this was and when I told her she said *"Oh, St Cecilia, she is the patron saint of music."*

All of a sudden, I remembered the violin my angel had presented to me and suddenly it felt as though I could begin to connect the dots. I searched for more information about St

Cecilia on the internet and was shocked to see an image of her depicted holding a violin. Before this conversation, I had never heard of St Cecilia or known anyone with that name. I printed out the picture of St Cecilia and placed it inside my angel journal. It took a bit of time and dedication to develop the connection. Thank goodness I had recorded these snippets of information in my journal so I could remember them, make connections and do some detective work. These small revelations gave me comfort that I was on the right track and beginning to channel angel messages in ways I had never expected.

4

THE WAYS OUR ANGELS COMMUNICATE WITH US

"No, I never saw an angel, but it is irrelevant
whether I saw one or not.
I feel their presence around me."

Paulo Coelho

Our angels communicate with us in so many different ways. What I bet you didn't know is that your angels have been communicating with you all your life and perhaps you didn't notice or never realised these were messages from them, intended for you personally.

So how do they do this? Here are some of the ways that our guardian angels give us signs they are looking out for us.

Angel numbers

Angels have their own Morse code. They communicate by showing us the same numbers over and over again. They also have a way of checking in with us by compelling us to look at the clock at a certain time; there will just happen to be a repeating number sequence for example: 16:16, 12:12 or 11:11

Have you ever been thinking about a certain problem or asking a question in your mind, then glanced at the clock and noticed repeating numbers? When this happens, look up the meaning of the number sequence. Very often this will give you a direct answer to the problem or question you were holding in your mind at that precise moment.

You may notice numbers on car license plates, on road signs, serial numbers or even on till receipts. As I was writing this book I was thinking about how I would typeset it. Getting the layout right was troubling me and I had no professional graphic design software or the time to learn how to use it. Right at that moment, an e-mail popped into my inbox. It was a speculative email from a company who specialise in creating eBooks and layouts and graphics for books. The time of the email was 12:22! I did have a little smile to myself and thanked my angel. Later on, I looked up the number meaning of 222 and found that it is linked to our divine life purpose and soul mission. It reminds us to keep up the good work and that everything will have positive results.

These things never cease to amaze me. I took it as a message not to give up if an obstacle such as the graphic design was getting in my way. My angels were telling me that my writing was important and to continue with it, they are there in the background helping me sort out the details. Things like this happen to me all the time; but not because I'm special or different. We all have an important life purpose and no one person's is better than another's. What does strike me is that I'm open and aware about all of this now and I notice these things a lot more. If this had occurred ten years ago I probably would have deleted the email without reading it because I was so 'busy' and carried on worrying. That is the thing about angelic connections, awareness brings with it wonderful help and guidance in exactly the ways we need and just when we need it. We will never be able to predict how and when it will come, but our angels are always there watching and helping us out.

Here are important messages associated with angel numbers:

Number 0

The number zero represents oneness. This number is giving you the message that you are at one with your angels and the divine. Be open to your intuition and trust that you have a direct connection with your angels. The number zero also signifies powerful new beginnings and that you have the power at your fingertips to initiate something that is part of your soul's journey.

Number 1

Stay positive. This number is all about releasing fears and being mindful about your thoughts. Our thoughts manifest things into our lives, so remember to keep them positive.

Number 2

This number is about belief. The angels have faith in whatever it is that you are doing or asking about so trust that you can do whatever it is you want.

Number 3

The number three is connected to the ascended masters, for example Jesus, Buddha, Quan Yin and other religious figures. This is a message that these powerful divine figures are helping you and sending their radiant energy and blessings with whatever you need help around.

Number 4

This is the angel number. It is the number the angels use to tell you that they have heard your prayers and they are working on your behalf to bring you what you have asked about and wished for.

Number 5

This is all about big changes which are always for our highest good. Ask your angels for help during this time of change. It also about releasing that which no longer serves us.

Number 6

This number is all about possessions, material things, home, family and stability. It is important not to worry about these things because worry is associated with lack and when we focus on what we lack then we attract more of the same. Be grateful for what you already have and stay balanced between spiritual and material abundance.

Number 7

This is the number of divine magic. When you see the number seven appearing continually then this is an affirmation from your angels that a miracle is on its way and they are opening up the doors of opportunity for you.

Number 8

This signifies the infinite supply of financial abundance, prosperity, time, ideas and whatever else you are looking to bring into your life. It is also connected to finding your life's purpose.

Number 9

This is the action number. Your angels are asking you to get to work on whatever you have been thinking about. You are ready so what are you waiting for?

Numbers after 9 contain a combination of the different elements of the single numbers. So for example, number 12 is a combination of the energies of number 1 and number 2. Seeing repeating number patterns such as 11, 22, and 333, 555,

777, etc. is very powerful. The energy is doubled or trebled so this is a like a big neon sign lighting up in relation to whatever numbers you are seeing.

Angel Symbols

White feathers

White feathers are the most well-known way for our angels to let us know they at around. The white feather is symbolic of their wings and white is the colour of purity, spirituality and divinity. Seeing a white feather is like a lovely hello from your guardian angel. It can also act as a way of affirming certain choices we are trying to make or giving us a resounding yes to a question we may have asked our Angels. People have told me many stories of how they have found white feathers and usually it is in the most unusual circumstances.

When I was first writing this section of the book I thought to myself *"Hmm, why don't my angels show me white feathers"* it's not a symbol they seem to share with me. The following morning I was coming down the stairs and on the staircase was a single, small white feather. It wasn't there the night before, my stair carpet is red and I would have seen it, it stood out so clearly. I love my angels; they definitely have a sense of humour.

Shapes

Your angels might show you their presence through symbols such as shapes, for example: pyramids; stars; hearts or butterfly shapes.

The way that the Angels communicate with me and my daughter is through heart shapes. I first began noticing what I call my 'angel hearts' when I broke up with Daniel four years ago.

For the first time since I was fifteen years old, on Valentine's Day I found myself alone without a boyfriend or husband. It was that very day that I began to notice the hearts. You may be thinking, *"Natalia it was Valentine's Day and there are hearts everywhere!"* Well, yes there were, but not in the way that you would imagine. Let me explain.

That morning I took the rubbish out to the bin in my garden. When I came back inside there was something stuck to the bottom of my shoe. When I looked it was a small plastic heart. I thought nothing of it, peeled it off my shoe and placed in the bin. I then went to the supermarket to do my shopping. I was fishing around in vegetable boxes for some large baking potatoes. The potato I pulled out was heart shaped. I was quite amused by this. *"What a coincidence"* I thought and then carried on with my shopping.

That day and the days that followed, I was seeing heart shapes all over the place. When I put a splodge of makeup onto my face in the morning, I looked in the mirror and the makeup had formed a heart shape. I saw heart-shaped puddles in the street, a heart shape in the foam on my cappuccino and a random heart in the polka dot pattern on the blouse I was wearing. These heart shapes were quite literally everywhere I turned.

I see all of this now as a loving message from my angels to tell me that I had made the right choice. That I wasn't alone and that I would never be without love because I am surrounded by it. It has also occurred to me that my angels use a heart shape because it looks like a pair of angel wings that are close together. Every time I see these random heart shapes in ways that are completely unexpected, I take this as a lovely *"hello"* from my angels and each time I look upwards and thank them dearly.

Symbolic Animals and Creatures

You may receive angel communication through seeing a certain animal, insect or bird. Often you will keep seeing this creature over and over again or the animal will behave in an odd way. They might cross your path or stare at you until you notice them and they will not be unafraid of you. These are very likely to be signs and symbols from your angels and it is worth looking into their symbolic meaning. Chances are this is the message your angels are trying to pass on to you.

Coins

When I was a child my mother always told me that when you find a coin in the street it is a sign from your angels. I often find coins and, whenever I do, I always smile and say *"Hello angels!"* I have read a lot of books written by angel intuitives and many of them mention finding coins as an angelic symbol.

You may find your angels communicate with you through leaving coins for you to discover. You might find them around your home, in strange places or in the street as you are walking along. I often find coins just after musing over a certain dilemma or asking a certain question in my mind.

I went to the local shop to buy some milk during a period of intensively writing this book. I always need to top up my coffee levels whilst I'm writing. I had been turning over a few ideas in my mind and I was wrestling with whether or not to share my personal story at the beginning of the book. I had written the first half of the book and my thoughts were gnawing away at me about whether to include my story. As I walked into the shop, I saw a bright, shiny five pence piece on the black welcome mat in the shop doorway. Several people had walked through and no one had seen the coin. It's as though it was reserved just for me. I smiled as I picked it up. The next day I went to meet a friend for breakfast. As I got out of the car, there at my feet was a two pence coin. I found three coins the following day on a trip to the cinema with my daughter. I took these coins sightings as an affirmation from my angels that it was safe for me to include my story; so that is what I did.

Instinct and intuition

Angel messages very frequently appear to us as flashes of inspiration or a strong sense of intuition. Intuition can be described as a sense of knowing; a feeling that you should take a particular action; you don't know why you should do it, but it just seems important. Then, when you follow your inner knowing by taking action, these actions can often result in something miraculous. Remember; miracles can be large or small but they are still miracles nonetheless.

So, that urge you had to leave the house at a certain time might result in you meeting someone who is to become an important person in your life. That feeling you get about going to a particular workshop or reading a particular book might contain a message that is critical in changing the direction of your life. Sometimes, the impact of these actions doesn't show itself for a while; but over time, it really does have positive and transformational consequences.

Following my intuition had a life-changing impact for me last year. I have never drawn or painted because at school I was constantly told I wasn't artistic or creative enough. I have always looked at people painting and drawing and yearned to be able to do this myself, but I told myself I shouldn't bother because I wasn't good enough.

Last year my daughter was going on holiday for two weeks over the summer. I had just finished a big work project and was ready to take some time off. I decided I wanted to have a little adventure and do something different but I wasn't sure what. As I was browsing Facebook one day, an advert came up for an artist called Alena Hennessy. Her style of artwork was so beautiful and I really loved the way that she painted. I decided to like her page. I left it at that and thought no more about it.

Then, as Alena began posting updates on her Facebook page, I would see them on my news feed. She lived in America and would post up beautiful images of the area where she lived and some of her latest work in progress. She also mentioned that she taught workshops. *"How wonderful it would be"* I thought to myself, *"to go and learn from Alena."* Where were these thoughts coming from? I couldn't paint and yet I found myself contemplating doing a painting workshop. I couldn't afford the time or the money to go to America; that was out of the question. So, I pushed those thoughts aside.

The evening after my daughter had gone away, I was on my own in the house. I was a little lonely and feeling bored and for some reason I couldn't get Alena Henessy and her beautiful paintings out of my mind. I decided to have a look at her website. Even if I couldn't afford to go to America, I could do a little daydreaming and see what kinds of workshops Alena was running. When I looked, lo and behold, Alena was actually coming to the UK the following week. She was teaching at an Art Retreat at Magdalene College, Oxford. The timing of the retreat was perfect, it was affordable and there was one space remaining. I jumped at the chance to go and without even thinking twice, I booked myself onto it right there and then.

The day before I was due to go on the retreat I was gripped by the familiar fear and doubt. I did consider changing my mind, but I'm so glad I summoned the courage to get in my car and go. What happened on that retreat was nothing short of magical.

I met an amazing group of people who were all so supportive and like-minded. We bonded over our love of all things spiritual and creative.

The three days of workshops consisted of meditations, lots of practical demonstrations of techniques and everyone helped one another through the sharing of ideas and materials. I learned to relax, reach my calm centre and to just let the paint go wherever my heart told it to. I began to unleash the artist that had been trapped inside me; the one that was scared of being a failure. I was now free to express myself artistically and it felt very good indeed. The most important thing was not the paintings themselves, but the fact that I had given myself permission to try this. I was not attached to the outcome, I just wanted to enjoy the process of painting.

When I returned home from the retreat, I continued painting and taking classes and I can honestly say, not a week has gone by without me picking up a paintbrush or doing a sketch. One year on, I am in the process of completing the paintings for my own deck of oracle cards. That is something that I never believed I was capable of doing. All of this affirms for me that when you trust your angels to guide you, listen to their messages through your inner voice and follow your intuition, they will always point you in the direction where you truly need to be.

Sometimes, our angels use the intuition of other people as a channel, to make sure we are in exactly the right place at the right time. I have experienced this many times, one of the best and most rewarding examples I can share with you, is one fateful New Years Eve a few years ago.

During the time that I was with Daniel, my friends did not like him at all so they avoided being around me. Daniel picked up on this and used it to his advantage. Slowly but surely, he weeded out my close friends. They didn't want to be around me when he was there, so, over time, my friends evaporated from my life.

One of my closest friends was Tracy. Her son was in the same class at school as my daughter. We had become so close because we lived just down the road from one and another and had so many things in common. We had both been married for seventeen years and our marriages broke up around the same time. My friendship with Tracy became a casualty of my relationship with Daniel and I didn't see or speak to her for two years.

The first New Year's Eve after he and I broke up I had my daughter Estella with me and I wanted us to go out and do something. She was too young to take out to a party, so I decided we would go to the cinema instead. My daughter just wanted to stay at home but I was adamant I did not want to stay in on this special night. I felt quite sad and wasn't particularly looking forward to the coming year, but I wanted to go out and do something to cheer myself up. We bickered a little bit about it, but she ended up agreeing to go.

Unbeknownst to me, Estella had been thinking about my friend Tracy and decided she wanted to wish her a happy New Year. My daughter did not have Tracy's number, so she searched around and managed to find the number because it was still programmed into my home telephone.

Estella texted Tracy and Tracy replied delighted to have received this text. Tracy asked how I was and what we were doing for New Year's Eve. My daughter told her we were going to see a particular film at the cinema. Tracy replied saying that she was also taking her daughter to the cinema that night. It turned out we were both going to be seeing the same film, at the same cinema at the same time.

When we walked into cinema and I saw Tracy again for the first time it was like we had never been apart. We hugged, chatted and laughed and went for dinner afterwards. That evening was the most perfect New Year's Eve. It went from being an evening where I was feeling sad and lost to bringing my beautiful friend back into my life. Tracy, me and our daughters made a pact to spend New Year's Eve together thereafter and most years we have managed to do it. We always have the best fun and laughter-filled times and we always thank our angels (and my little earth angel Estella) for bringing us back to together.

Messages through words and music

Our angels often pass on their wisdom and guidance through the lyrics in songs. You might be thinking of a certain dilemma that you have or a question you really want an answer to and then the affirmation of that comes through the next song that plays on the radio. Other times you will read the answer to your question in a magazine article, in the words written in an advertisement or even on the side of a bus.

I remember very clearly having a mental tussle with myself about whether to invest in creating the Angel Wisdom Programme. I wasn't sure about whether it was the right thing to do, *"Would anyone be interested in it? I want to do it very professionally and it's going to take a lot of time and money. I don't have either of these resources in abundance right now."* I said to myself. I wasn't sure what to do, but I couldn't get the concept of this programme out of my mind. My heart seemed to be telling me to go for it but my rational mind was telling me all the reasons why I shouldn't. I was also having doubts about my knowledge and ability to do this. So, as I often do at times like these, I turned to my trusty angel cards. I picked up my Kyle Gray Angel Prayers card deck. The card that

I drew was *"Look for signs from heaven"*. Okay angels I thought to myself, let's see what you have to tell me.

The day after my soul searching and questioning, I was at a conference. There were around 100 of us attending this conference and we were each given a raffle ticket with a number on it. The prize was a goody bag filled with art materials. My number was drawn and I was delighted to be the lucky winner. When I looked inside the bag, one of the products was a stencil. The words on the stencil said:

"Why not now listen to your inner voice you really can do whatever you want"

I was so happy to read this; it had answered my question beautifully. On the way home from the conference there were some road works, so the traffic was moving very slowly. My mind started to wander as my car began to grind to a halt and I looked up into the sky in front of me. There, just ahead was a magnificent cloud formation in the shape of a huge pair of angel wings. If the words of the stencil sent confirmation enough then this was a loud and clear yes from the Universe. So here I am following through on their message, putting my faith in the angels and their wise guidance.

Cloud Formations

Do you remember as a child looking for images in the clouds? When I was five years old I went to a lovely village school in the small town where I grew up. The summers seemed endless and this school had the most magnificent playing fields. My friends and I used to run down to the playing fields at lunchtime. We'd turn cartwheels, sit making daisy chains and wish on dandelion clocks. Afterwards we would lie down on the grass and look up at the clouds to see what we could see within them. I remember seeing faces, crocodiles, dragons and all kinds of weird and wonderful things in those clouds.

We may not have all time in the world to cloud watch like we did when we were children, but our angels can often send us messages through cloud formations, so it's always worth taking a quick look at the sky and seeing what you notice. If your angels have a message for you then they will give you nudge to lift your head upwards and see the cloud shape they have for you, just like they did for me with my angel wings cloud.

You may be reading this and thinking *"My angels never give me signs"* well all you have to do is ask them. Take a moment to close your eyes and in your mind or out loud ask your angels *"Angels show me a sign and help me to notice this sign"*. Then wait and watch!

Earth Angels

Throughout the course of our lives people are sent to us to mentor, guide and teach us. These people show up in our lives at the precise moment when we are ready to receive their wisdom. It's like that old saying "When the student is ready the teacher appears." That is the phenomena that I call 'earth angels'. These people who show up in our lives aren't actual angels, but they are doing divine work and they help us in ways that we may not see or understand at the time. I believe there are three different types of earth angels and they all come in different guises.

The Fairy Godmother

These people are the kindly, wise teachers or friends whom we fall in love with instantly. For example, think of Cinderella and her Fairy Godmother; how the Fonze from Happy Days took awkward and geeky Ritchie Cunningham under his wing. These are the people who push us to do and achieve things, they are the people who see potential in us; offer us peace and safety and believe in us more than we believe in ourselves.

The Guru

The gurus are those people who are very experienced; they are placed in our lives to teach us. They have our best interests at heart just like the fairy godmothers but their role is not to be warm and loving. Their purpose is to nudge and cajole us along by giving us tough love, so that we can step into our power. They will annoy us, prod us, push our buttons and make us work hard on ourselves. Until we make those all-important life changes and learn those critical lessons. For examples of gurus, think of Yoda's relationship with Luke Skywalker and Mr Miyagi's mentoring of the Karate Kid.

The Bad Guy

The last category of earth angels is the bad guys; those people who treat us with out-and-out distain and cruelty. They are the people are there to hold a mirror up to us or to wake us up and move us along if we have outstayed a particular habit or part of our journey. Their role is not to do this in a pleasant or polite way. Their purpose is to shock us, make us feel incredibly uncomfortable and yet at the same time they force us to realise that now is make or break. How long can we stay in this place of discomfort? It's often incredibly painful to move on, but we do it. Eventually the pain stops and the wounds heal. If you remain in a place of pain, the pain will go on and on and on.

Throughout my own life I have come across so many different earth angels. My fairy godmothers have been my English teacher, Mr McKenzie whose inspirational teaching and unfailing belief in me gave me the confidence to take English

A Level and to believe in my writing ability. My cousin Moises and the lady named Chavella who was my aunt's house cleaner. They were the only people I could confide in when I lived in Mexico and they offered me a shoulder to cry on and so much comfort during those tough times. My boss Ken Thomas who pushed me forward at work and did everything he could to help me get noticed and promoted, even though it meant he would lose me. My wonderful friends Tracy, Andrew and Laura, who have held my hand and supported me during the most testing times in recent years.

One of the most powerful gurus I have come across is a lady called Julie Starr. I met Julie during the time when I worked a business consultant. Julie is a highly respected business coach and hired me to work on a big project. This involved extensive travel back and forth to Prague and Arizona. Julie could see I was like a square peg in a round hole with what I was doing with my life at the time. She didn't fall for any of the charm and nonsense that beguiled other people; she saw right through me and had a way of prodding me and asking me questions that made squirm. I have to be honest and say that at the time I did not like her one bit. She was all about honesty and I was all about putting on a mask. The more she tried to get me to uncover what was beneath the mask, the tighter I held on to it.

Julie was put into my life for a reason and she would remain there until I had learned what she had to teach me. Whilst at times I was incredibly angry with her, I could not avoid the truth. We had some very vocal differences of opinion, one that even involved us being pulled over by a traffic cop in Arizona. We were driving to the airport in a rental car and screaming at each other so loudly. She lost her concentration, forgot she was in the USA and ended up making an unlawful manoeuvre! That was to be the first of quite a few arguments and disagreements we would have. Julie said to me *"You have told yourself you are not lovable so at some point in your life you decided if you could not have love you would take respect in its place."* How right she was. I see it all now, but Julie Starr was the person that would begin the process of peeling back the layers and help me face up to it. I thank Julie for her wisdom and for always speaking the truth. Today, I am glad to say, we are very dear friends and I now greatly value rather than fear her opinions. She is also an immensely-talented writer and continues to dispense her wisdom through her books.

I have mentioned a major bad guy in my life, Daniel. Well, he turned out to be an earth angel (albeit in wolf's clothing) and I thank him for what he did. He helped me break a pattern and begin the process of reclaiming my self worth. There have been quite a few people since Daniel who have played the bad guy earth angels in my life. Their actions have steered me towards a much more fulfilling place. It is very difficult to find anything positive when we are at the receiving end of the bad guys' behaviour, but time will always help us see that what they did was for our greater good. Their actions teach us important lessons. They change the way we think, they make us move on to better things and it is often through life's struggles and our darkest times that we are transformed.

We aren't just on the receiving end of earth angels; we are often placed in the role of earth angel ourselves. At some point in your life you have been or will be someone's fairy godmother, guru or even someone's bad guy at least once. Look forward to meeting the future fairy godmothers, gurus and bad guys on your pathway. Bless each and every one of them for the unique roles they will play in helping you achieve your life purpose.

Take a moment to think about the fairy godmothers, gurus and bad guys in your life and how have they helped you.

My Fairy Godmothers:

How they have helped me:

My Gurus:

How they have helped me:

My Bad Guys:

How they have helped me:

5

ANGEL AFFIRMATIONS

"Kind words are the music of the world.
They have a power which seems to be
beyond natural causes,
as if they were some angel's song..."

Frederick William Fraser

I was first introduced to the concept of affirmations when I read Louise L Hay's book 'Heal Your Life'. What she spoke of in that wonderful book was not only simple but it was life changing for me.

So what are affirmations and why are they so special? The meaning of the word affirmation is "the action or process of confirming something." Louise Hay tells us how to create positive affirmations, statements that we think and say that act like energy we put out to Universe. These words are so powerful that they attract to us whatever we are thinking about and saying. You may have heard of 'The Secret' and the 'Law of Attraction'. Affirmations are a similar concept to these, but Louise Hay was talking about them long before they were well-known or fashionable.

We make affirmations all the time without even realising. I hear people making affirmations every day of the week, in casual conversations, in meetings, in emails I receive. I'll give you an example. I met a friend for coffee recently and she was talking about the lack of romance in her life. The words she used were "There are no decent single men. I will never meet a man without going on internet dating." Right then and there she was creating an affirmation that the Universe will honour. What is worse is that she probably thinks this regularly too. Chances are she is affirming it over and over again in her mind.

What the Universe hears is she does not want to meet decent single men anywhere other than through internet dating. And so it is. When I read Louise Hay's book I was shocked at just how many affirmations I was making that were keeping me 'stuck' and maintaining and bringing me more of what I felt was lacking in my life. It was only then that I realised I needed to change, not just what I said but also what I thought. Our thoughts are just as powerful as any words that are spoken.

Be very careful indeed with your words and thoughts because they can have a much bigger impact than you may realise. I remember in the early days of running my business being very concerned about cash flow. I had quite a large invoice to pay to a supplier and I was worried that I would not get paid in time by my own customers, before my supplier began asking me for the money. The thought crossed my mind *"I hope they don't ask me for payment yet."* Lo and behold, within half an hour the supplier was on the phone calling me to collect payment. I'm sure this has happened to you at some point. We attract what we think about. So my thoughts *"ask me for payment"* were what the Universe heard and it brought me exactly what I was thinking about.

So I'm going to share some affirmations with you that I hear nearly every day or read on social media. How many do you use regularly or have you used any of these today I wonder? We're only human; I still do it too, even though I know all about positive affirmations. I have become adept at correcting my thoughts immediately as soon as I realise what I've done.

Turning a negative affirmation into a positive one takes daily practice and regular mindfulness and effort, but it can be done and eventually it will become second nature to you. Soon, you will even bristle at the very mention of a negative affirmation!

Here are some common affirmations I hear every day. How many of these have you used lately?

- *I hate my job/my boss.*
- *I'm in a dead-end job.*
- *I have no direction in life.*
- *I'm underpaid.*
- *I feel fed up.*
- *No one appreciates me.*
- *People only get in touch when they want something.*
- *I'm overweight.*
- *I can't stop eating unhealthy food.*
- *I can't stop smoking.*
- *I need a glass of wine.*
- *I hate my body.*
- *I don't want to be unhappy.*
- *I'm sick and tired of everything.*
- *I'm in constant pain.*
- *I'm lonely.*
- *I can't find a man/woman to love me.*
- *I can't cope.*
- *I feel stuck.*
- *Life is so challenging.*
- *I never have any money.*

And the list could go on and on (in fact typing those things was making me feel very uncomfortable indeed).

So if you truly do want angelic support and guidance, if you want with all your heart the Universe to conspire to help you, you're going to have to help yourself by changing your affirmations to positive ones.

An effective positive affirmation is always stated in the present tense. As though what we would like to bring into our lives is already in motion, just like the Universe. When we ask for things in the future tense it is like a plea, which again is coming from a place of lack. It is also convincing our subconscious mind that these things are out of our reach and we will never get there.

So here are some new affirmations for the things we discussed earlier. Try these on for size and see how they fit:

- I am open to a brilliant new career that fits my skills and talents perfectly.
- Golden opportunities are everywhere for me.
- My path in life is a series of stepping stones to even greater success.
- I learn from every experience.
- All is well in my world.
- Love is everywhere; I am loving and I am lovable.
- I am truly blessed.
- I am divinely guided and protected.
- I make choices that are beneficial for me.
- All my needs and desires are being met.
- I am totally open to the flow of abundance and prosperity.
- I choose to be healthy and free.
- I listen to what my body tells me.

- I am healthy, whole and complete.
- The past is over I am at peace.
- I love and approve of myself.
- I choose to love and enjoy myself.
- I am powerful and capable.
- I know I am worthwhile.
- Letting go is easy.

All of the above affirmations are examples from Louise Hay's book 'You can Heal Your Life'. Some of them you may feel more comfortable in saying than others. I have included them to help get you thinking about ways in which you can create new affirmations for yourself. Use these or create your own that use language that fits best with who you are. Most of all, practice turning your thoughts and words into positive

Create your own positive affirmations here.

My positive affirmations:

6

HAVE COMPASSION – IT'S NEVER JUST ABOUT A PAIR OF JEANS

*"…don't judge my book by the chapter
you walked in on"*

Matthew Linback

This may seem like a strange title for a chapter, but ever since I witnessed a certain incident a couple of years ago, I have wanted to write about it. Now that time has come.

In the UK there are a chain of shops called M&S. They sell high quality clothes, shoes, gifts, home wares and food. I was browsing around the M&S store in the town where I live when I noticed a pretty scarf and decided to buy it. As I waited to pay, there was a lady at the cash desk who was already being served.

The store was very quiet because it was nearly closing time, so I could hear everything that was being said at the cash desk. The lady in front of me was returning a pair of navy coloured jeans. When she washed them, the dye from the jeans had leaked out onto her other, lighter coloured clothes and ruined them.

The shop assistant turned the jeans inside out to find the washing instructions label. She proudly announced that the washing instructions stated "This item is colourfast - please wash separately." That is when the discussion between the owner of the jeans and the shop assistant started to get very heated. The customer was becoming irate, both at the fact that she hadn't seen the instructions on this tiny label and at the fact that the shop assistant was making her look rather foolish in front of the other members of the staff at the cash desk.

The customer became insistent that she had never had any problems before when washing jeans and that the label was too small to notice. At that moment, another two members of staff moved in to support their colleague in berating the customer – saying things like *"well, it's obvious isn't it? Who doesn't check the label for instructions?"* It was fascinating to watch their behaviour as they effectively flanked their team mate and ganged up on the customer. Suddenly, the customer lost her cool completely, picked up the jeans and flung them at the shop assistant. She stood there for a few minutes, shouting at the top of her voice and was on the verge of tears, before storming out of the shop.

As I stepped forward to pay for my scarf, the shop assistant who had been at the centre of this incident looked at me in bewilderment and said *"Well, she's only got herself to blame. How ridiculous to wash dark coloured jeans for the first time with light coloured clothes!"* I just looked back at her and calmly said *"All of that wasn't about a pair of jeans."* The shop assistant stared at me in a bemused way and said *"Sorry I don't know what you mean."*

"Well" I replied *"she got angry with you over the jeans but it was about more than that. Sometimes, there are bigger things going on in a person's life. It's the smaller things like this push us over the edge. It wasn't the pair of jeans she was angry about, it was something much bigger."* What I was saying clearly went right over the shop assistant's head because she proceeded to continue gossiping with her

colleagues about the dramatic confrontation she had just had with this customer. About how the customer was wrong and she was right.

So what was happening here? Well, first of all I'm convinced that the lady with the jeans was experiencing some issues at the time of this showdown at the cash desk. What makes someone lash out and shout and scream in public? Perhaps it was a catalogue of events that have happened throughout her life. Maybe it was some life crisis she was coping with at the time. We often valiantly struggle on, showing a brave face to the world about the big things that we are dealing with; yet we lose control of our temper when someone jumps the queue in front of us at the supermarket. How often have you gotten angry when you are talking to someone on the telephone in a call centre or when you are driving and another driver makes an unexpected manoeuvre? Perhaps you have been on the receiving end of someone else's road rage? I know I certainly have and these are all outlets for the anger, the pain, the loss and the despair that we are carrying around inside of us.

Very often, confrontations like these are generated through fear. This situation escalated because it became all about proving who was right. The shop assistant had a fear of being wrong and needing to give a refund for the jeans. The customer had a fear of being made to look foolish in front of me and the shop assistants. If this had been handled with love and compassion instead of fear, the outcome would certainly have been a whole lot different. What I would like you to consider here is that the answer to everything is love and compassion.

The next time you find yourself in a situation where someone is getting angry with you, lashing out at you or complaining, or maybe all three. Ask yourself three things:

"What are they afraid of?"

"What is going on in their life that I do not know about?"

"How can I be more compassionate?"

In the example above, the lady with the jeans was afraid of looking foolish. This is exactly how the shop assistant and her colleagues made her feel. Maybe she really was not in a position to offer a refund for the jeans. What she could have done is be more sympathetic to the customer's plight. I'm sure we have all made mistakes at some point when washing clothes. (I remember putting a very expensive cashmere sweater in the dryer – it turned into a beautiful cashmere sweater fit for a Barbie doll to wear!) She could also have suggested a way the customer could sort out the damaged clothes. There are different products on the market that will remove dye from washed clothes and 'colour catchers' that will prevent this from happening in the future.

I am not condoning venting anger and frustration, nor am I saying this is okay if there is an excuse for it. What I am saying is this; instead of responding with anger and frustration, let's see how compassion works instead. Our angels have compassion for us. They see everything we do. They see the good things and the not so good things. They do not turn away from us, chastise us or judge us for our behaviour. They continue to love us, just as we are.

So how about if we all tried out a little earthly angelic behaviour, I wonder what a difference it would make? If just once a day everyone responded with love and compassion instead of fear, I'm convinced the world would be a much different and more loving place.

How can you be more compassionate in your own life?

Who can you have more compassion for?

Whose life story can you try to understand better rather than focusing on the 'chapter' you are both in right now?

7

CONNECTING WITH THE POWERFUL ENERGY OF THE ARCHANGELS

*"The warmth of an angel's light can comfort
and illuminate the whole world"*

You may have heard of the term archangel and be familiar with some of the archangel names, but who are these angels and how can they help you?

The archangels are believed to have been the very first angels created by God or whatever you consider to be 'the divine' and they are said to be the highest ranking angels that exist. The word archangel is derived from the Greek words 'Arche' which means ruler and 'Angelos' which means messenger. So if angels are messengers, then the archangels are the ruling messengers, the most powerful ones. Each archangel was given important responsibilities to do their work in both the heavenly and earthly dimensions.

The first Angels said to have been created by the divine are Michael, Raphael and Gabriel. There are references to archangels in different world religions such as Judaism, Christianity and Islam. Whilst the different religions don't agree on the details about archangels they do acknowledge their existence and their incredible power.

There are many different archangels, so as not to confuse you; I have decided to focus on just three of them.

So let me introduce you to my three favourite Archangels. Why are they my favourites? Well, they each have a special purpose and certain powers that align with the major things I am asked about during my angel readings. These Archangels can help us with key life stages and often align themselves with us during critical phases of our lives, even if we haven't asked for their help. Archangels and angels can be in many different places at the same time. Only earth operates within time and space, archangels and angels do not have the boundaries of time. That is why when we ask our angels for something it might take a few hours, days or weeks to happen. On the other hand it could take years to manifest. This is because the angels have no concept of time! Never worry about asking the Archangels for help or that you are taking up their valuable resources, they can be with a million people or more all the same time if necessary. So ask for and accept their guidance, strength, healing and support.

Archangel Michael (name meaning: "Who is like the Divine")

Archangel Michael is the leader of all the angels and archangels. He is both mentally and physically strong. His role is protection, courage, strength, truth and integrity. His main purpose is to rid the world and its inhabitants of the toxins associated with fear. Michael carries a sword that he uses to cut through etheric cords. He is often depicted wearing a cloak which is used to protect us from negative energy. The light Michael emits is brilliant, electric blue.

We all have chakras located within certain points in our body, these are the energy centres. Each chakra has etheric chords protruding from it. These cords look a little bit like rubber tubing. When we come in contact with people or have relationships with people these etheric chords extend to their chakras and vice versa. Fear within our relationships forms these chords. This can be fear of abandonment, co-dependency, attachments, unforgiveness, etc. Etheric cords act like hoses, so the energy goes back and forth between the people we are 'corded' with. What then happens is if the person we are corded to is experiencing stress or life challenges, that person will siphon energy from you. Sometimes you can quite literally feel it when you are around certain people. You may also be unwittingly doing this to others. It is important to ask Archangel Michael to come along and cut these etheric cords so that we are no longer attached. When Michael cuts these cords it does not mean we are no longer connected, will break up or experience detachment from these people. Remember, the etheric cords are created through fear. In cord cutting we are releasing the fear and stopping the energy drain from occurring.

When to call upon Archangel Michael:

- To help you follow and speak your truth.
- To help with stressful work deadlines.
- When you have an addiction.
- When you are suffering from nightmares.
- When you are having problems with electrical equipment, technology, when your car breaks down, etc.
- If you are suffering from a degenerative disease or terminal illness.
- To help you boost your self-esteem and sense of self-worth.
- To help motivate you.

- To cut the etheric cords between you and other people.

Archangel Michael is a very significant Archangel. The work he does is so powerful and important, you can and should call him in regularly to help clear and strengthen you; a bit like calling in a personal trainer, house keeper or security guard.

You will know when Archangel Michael is near when:

- *New opportunities to expand occur for you in the areas of career; finances or your life's work.*
- *Some one comes into your life and acts as a mentor. Chances are they are being guided and channelled by Archangel Michael.*
- *Things that no longer serve you fall away from your life. Michael is all about letting go of old energy. You feel compelled to leave old friendships behind you; begin de-cluttering your home or office space or admit to yourself that a goal you once wanted needs to be released.*

A Meditation for Etheric Cord Cutting with Archangel Michael

First of all find a comfortable place to sit or lie down. It is entirely up to you how you are positioned during this meditation; the most important thing is that you are comfortable.

So now that you are settled and comfortable I'd like to ask you close your eyes and relax.

Now take a deep breath in through your nose and as you breathe in take the breath all the way down to your belly so that your belly inflates as you inhale. Now breathe out and as you breathe out imagine that the breath is taking away all of your cares, thoughts and worries. You are safe here

---

in this moment, just keep taking deep breaths in. If any thoughts come into your mind let them go and bring your concentration back to your breathing.

Now imagine that there are roots growing out of the soles of your feet and travelling down, deep into the earth. These roots are keeping you safe and secure and as the roots travel down into the earth's core imagine that a beautiful white light is travelling up the roots through your feet and up through the whole of your body, cleansing you and bathing you in peace and serenity.

I'm going to invite Archangel Michael to stand above you and to place his hands above your head; the powerful blue light he emits is radiant and so intensely blue it is magnificent. The power of his blue light is so strong, Michael's blue light cascades all around you sealing your body in a protective bubble, cleansing your aura and holding you safely so that nothing can harm you. Now, invite Archangel Michael to take his sword and to cut through all of the etheric cords in each of your chakras. He is cutting through the cords that have attached to your chakras and connect you to other people. He is working his way around the chakras all over your body, cutting them away with a clean sweep of his sword, so that your energy can no longer be drained.

Archangel Michael is now burning away the end of each of the cords with a flame from the fire of unconditional love. Any connections that were once there through cords with yourself and others are now replaced with beautiful and unconditional love.

Imagine the chakra on the top of your head opening like the lid of a jar. Archangel Michael is pouring his beautiful blue, healing and cleansing light through your open crown chakra. The blue light travels down your face, along your neck, down through your chest, arms and along your fingers. His blue light is filling up your body. It continues to travel along your torso, down through your hips, to your legs, knees, calves, ankles and along your feet right down to your toes.

The blue light is scanning your whole body, seeking out any negativity and dissolving and melting it away. He is filling up the gaps where the negativity was sitting with his blue light, replacing the negativity with unconditional love and compassion; filling you with powerful energy.

Imagine the chakra on the top of your head closing tightly now so that you can remain protected and keep all of the goodness from Michael's bright blue light inside of you.

Archangel Michael keeps you within this bubble of light and blesses you as he leaves, so that you will remain protected now and thereafter this meditation.

I want you begin to become aware of being in the room again. Begin to slowing move your fingers and toes. Become aware of any noises you may hear. When you are ready gently open your eyes.

Archangel Raphael (Name meaning: "The Divine has healed")

Raphael's name is derived from the Hebrew word 'rapha' which means doctor or healer. Raphael is a powerful healer and is known as the physician angel. He helps us to heal our mind, body and spirit. The light Raphael emits is sparkling emerald green.

He is a sweet, kind, loving and gentle angel and is known for having a wonderful sense of humour!

His other responsibilities include helping travellers stay safe on their journeys and also assisting us on our spiritual journey, giving guidance and helping us see the truth. Raphael can help us heal from physical, emotional and mental pain; he also helps us heal from past lives. Raphael can help us unite with things we have lost and with people, including our soul mate.

When to call upon Archangel Raphael:

- To help relieve physical, emotional or mental pain.
- To help heal you from any physical ailments.
- To protect you during travel.
- If you are studying as a practitioner or practicing in any medical field.
- To help guide you along your spiritual journey.
- To help you connect with your soul mate in this lifetime.

Signs that Archangel Raphael is around you:

- *Seeing sparkling green lights when you are meditating or feeling very relaxed.*
- *Seeing his name in unusual places.*
- *Feeling heat, tingling or vibrations.*
- *Noticing advertisements, books or magazines about health or articles to do with remedies connected with an ailment you might have.*

I had a very bad tooth abscess a couple of years ago and I was in so much pain. I had to run a jewellery making workshop at a location that was three hours drive away and I would be staying overnight. The infection in my tooth flared up so badly I was in agony. I set off early in the morning to get there and had to park my car at the side of the road for a while. I could not concentrate on driving because of the pain. As I lay there in agony in the back seat of my car I prayed to Archangel Raphael for help.

I managed to get back in the driver's seat and finish the journey. I soldiered on with running my workshop until just before lunch time when I could stand the pain no longer. I asked one of the ladies in the office if she could recommend a local dentist I could contact for an emergency appointment. She printed out a list of dentists for me and I rang the first one.

The receptionist who answered my call said she could fit me in but it would not be until the very end of the day. I accepted the appointment, then, within two minutes of ending the call, she rang me back. She told me *"That was so bizarre. Another patient called straight after you and cancelled their appointment. Can you come over in 15 minutes? You can have their appointment."* Thank goodness for Archangel Raphael. I was able to have some emergency treatment and was well enough within the hour to return and run the rest of my workshop.

After that, I meditated a great deal with Archangel Raphael and when the time came to have my tooth removed, I was talking to him in my mind throughout the whole procedure; asking him for help and healing.

The day after my tooth was extracted; my dentist actually telephoned me to see if I was feeling okay. I was quite shocked as I have never before or since experienced a dentist giving direct after care in this way, to a patient. I bless Archangel Raphael for taking care of me during this time.

A guided healing meditation with Archangel Raphael

First of all find a comfortable place to sit or lie down. It is entirely up to you how you are positioned during this meditation; the most important thing is that you are comfortable.

So now that you are settled and comfortable close your eyes and relax.

Take a deep breath in through your nose and as you breathe in, take the breath all the way down to your belly so that your belly inflates as you inhale. Now breathe out and as you breathe out imagine that the breath is taking away all of your cares, thoughts and worries. You are safe here in this moment, just keep taking deep breaths in. If any thoughts come into your mind let them go and bring your concentration back to your breathing.

Now imagine that there are roots growing out of the souls of your feet and travelling down, deep into the earth. These roots are keeping you safe and secure and as the roots travel down into the earth's core. Imagine that a beautiful white light is travelling up the roots through your feet and up through the whole of your body, cleansing you and bathing you in peace and serenity.

Imagine that you are in a beautiful garden. You are sitting in a beautifully soft chair and you are so comfortable. The flowers are in full bloom and there is vibrant green grass everywhere. The sun is beating down on you but it is gently keeping your warm. There is no discomfort from the sun whatsoever, you just feel safe, warm and happy.

You can hear the gentle melodic singing of the birds and some water trickling from a nearby stream. All is well. As you look across the garden a beautiful green light appears in the distance, the light is magnificent and it begins to sparkle and glow. The light grows bigger and bigger until it expands and covers everything around you and begins to envelop you too. You feel very safe within this light as if it has injected energy, warmth and healing vibrations throughout your body and given you an even deeper sense of well-being. The source of this light is Archangel Raphael and he appears in front of you smiling and happy, arms outstretched and delighted to see and be with you.

Thank Archangel Raphael for being here with you and for bathing you in his beautiful emerald green, sparkling light. Say these words either out loud or in your mind:

"Thank you Raphael for healing my body, for nurturing and protecting me. For keeping me safe and well; for making me whole and giving me strength. Thank you for your loving kindness"

Now allow Raphael to send his green light swirling around your body protecting you and sealing you within this magical bubble of green light.

Imagine you crown chakra at the top of your head opening like a flower. Raphael pours his green light into your chakra and down into your body. As the green light cascades down through every part of your body it clears and balances your chakras and heals every cell. Sit with this green light and allow Raphael to do his work, enjoy receiving this loving healing. It is Raphael's honour to help you and to heal and support you.

Imagine the chakra on the top of your head closing tightly again so that you can remain protected and keep all of the goodness of Raphael's healing green light inside of you.

Archangel Raphael keeps you within this bubble of green light and blesses you as he leaves, so that you will remain protected now and thereafter this meditation.

Now begin to become aware of being in the room again. Begin to slowly move your fingers and toes. Become aware of any noises you may hear. When you are ready gently open your eyes.

Archangel Gabriel (Name meaning: "The Divine is my strength")

Gabriel is depicted as a female archangel in art and literature and she is known as the messenger. All angels are messengers, but Gabriel has a leading role in this. The light Gabriel emits is sparkling and golden.

Gabriel can bring you messages, so if you are looking for answers to questions, as well as your own guardian angel, she is the archangel to call upon. Gabriel is often depicted holding a trumpet; this signifies her role as messenger and announcer of news. She is most well-known for having visited the Virgin Mary and Elizabeth, to tell them the news of Jesus' and John the Baptist's births.

Gabriel is the messenger angel; hence she helps anyone who is involved with communication, writing, speaking and the arts. She helps us find our true calling and will help you understand your life purpose. She is also a powerful angel to call upon to help with fertility, conceiving a baby and adoption.

When to call upon Archangel Gabriel:

- When you need help with clarity and confidence with a writing, speaking, communication, artistic, creative project.
- If you have writers block.
- When you are feeling lost and looking for your life's purpose.
- If you are thinking of moving house or changing career.
- When you need divine inspiration and motivation.
- When you would like to conceive or adopt a child.
- To help give birth to a plan or idea.

Signs that Archangel Gabriel is around you:

- *Seeing an increase in emails or mail correspondence – she is the messenger angel after all! Look at the common themes within these messages; she may be trying to tell you to focus on something in particular, so pay attention.*
- *You may feel inclined to do more reading and research.*
- *Hearing car horns or whistles with increased frequency – Gabriel is often depicted carrying a trumpet to herald news, so she uses these modern forms of heraldry to grab our attention.*

I have to add something here. While I was writing this book I did most of my work on it in the evenings and at weekends. At the mid-point of this project I would spend all of my free time intensively writing. I noticed that a child, who lives a few doors away down the street, was playing outside and blowing a whistle constantly. As I was finishing the book the weather had been very warm and sunny. This child had been blowing the whistle for hours on end. Apart from slightly annoying me I didn't think anything of it. That is until I was proof reading and editing this section!

Archangel Gabriel works with writers and creatives, so I do feel she has been with me, giving me inspiration and encouraging me to dedicate myself to this task and to complete it.

A guided meditation with Archangel Gabriel for inspiration

First of all find a comfortable place to sit or lie down. It is entirely up to you how you are positioned during this meditation; the most important thing is that you are comfortable.

Now that you are settled and comfortable, close your eyes and relax.

Now take a deep breath in through your nose and as you breathe in take the breath all the way down to your belly so that your belly inflates as you inhale. Now breathe out and as you breathe out imagine that the breath is taking away all of your cares, thoughts and worries. You are safe here in this moment, just keep taking deep breaths in. If any thoughts come into your mind let them go and bring your concentration back to your breathing.

Ask the archangel Gabriel to step into your aura. Feel her beautiful warm, nurturing energy and golden light.

Now say either out loud or in your mind the following words:

"Thank Gabriel for guiding me and helping me to hear your divine messages. Thank you for helping me to follow your guidance and fulfil my life's purpose.

Thank you for clearing away any confusion and giving me the wisdom I need to make good decisions and the ability to act on those decisions with confidence.

Thank you for helping me to conceive my true heart's desire. I am open to receiving your divine creativity and blessings."

Now visualise what it is that you would like Archangel Gabriel to help you conceive. See yourself doing whatever is your heart's desire, sense how it feels to have this manifest for you. Capture the image and feelings of what you have visualised and place them in a gold bubble. Imagine the bubble floating upwards into the Universe and up into heaven where what you would like to conceive receives highest Divine blessing. Now the bubble containing your heart's desire floats back down, down and down until it reaches your aura. What you would like to conceive is so full of wonderful divine energy it cannot be contained in the bubble any longer. The bubble bursts and your heart's desires turn into a shower of golden glitter that flows all around your aura.

Archangel Gabriel blesses you as she begins to drift away and leaves you surrounded by her golden light. Just stay within the place of love, peace and stillness for a few moments knowing that what you have wished for has been divinely blessed.

Now begin to become aware of being in the room again. Begin to slowly move your fingers and toes. Become aware of any noises you may hear. When you are ready gently open your eyes.

8

ABOUT FEAR AND BREATHING

*"Ultimately we know deeply that the other
side of fear is freedom"*

Marilyn Ferguson

I mentioned in Chapter 4 about the concept of earth angels. Well, another earth angel gurus I want to tell you about is a man called Mark Abadi. He is a very rare soul and I feel lucky to have crossed paths with him. He describes himself as a holistic therapist, spiritual teacher and explorer of consciousness. It is remarkable being in his presence because he has this deep sense of knowing and says just the right thing to touch the core of you; it is as if he can see right through you.

Four years ago I came across Mark through a spiritual network he was running in Manchester. I had reached my lowest ebb a few months previously and was beginning the long climb upwards, just around the time that I met him. I decided to invest in some spiritual coaching sessions with him. I only needed three of these, they were so powerful.

Going through those sessions was hard work. We didn't talk about Natalia the career person, the mother, daughter, friend, ex-girlfriend, ex-wife, failure. We talked about the real Natalia. He asked me to imagine if I had no name; no gender and no age. *"Who would you be then?"* he asked. When we are attached to an identity, like I was, you live your life in fear. Fear that it might be taken away from you; fear that people will not like you; fear that your mask might slip and people will see you for who you truly are; fear that who you are is not enough; fear of being alone. The funny thing about hitting rock bottom is there is nothing left to fear. The things that I was most scared of had actually happened to me. I was still there, alive and kicking. Things felt very strange, that's for sure, but after the storm all that was left was an eerie sense of calm.

My sessions with Mark were instrumental in me learning to see and love myself for who I was. The most memorable thing he said to me was this:

"Natalia, you are not wrong or right; good or bad; perfect or imperfect. You just are and in this moment everything is just as it should be."

One of the simplest and most important things I learned from Mark Abadi was how to breathe. He noticed that my breathing was very shallow. He explained that we often breathe into the top of our chest. With the busy and stressful lives we all lead nowadays, a lot of stress builds up in our bodies and we hold the pressure and stress in the top third of our bodies.

He explained that our power sits right at the base of the body, so when we breathe we really need to breathe all the way down into the belly.

So let's practice this right now:

- Breathe in through your nose and take the breath right down into the lowest part of your belly
- Inflate your belly as you breathe in, so that it expands as far as it can

- Exhale and as you exhale, breathe out through your mouth
- As you breathe out your stomach deflates again

How did that feel?

What did you observe while doing this and afterwards?

When we are fearful about something, the fear sits inside our belly. Have you ever experienced nervous knots in your stomach? That is the adrenaline from fear building up inside of you.

Breathing deeply when you are anxious or afraid helps to expel the anxiety and fear along with the stale air. Have the courage to breathe deeply into the core of your body; to be full and complete; to face the fear and release it. Breathing this way really will change your life.

PART II

HOW TO WORK WITH ANGEL CARDS

*"Angels are speaking to all of us...some
of us are just listening better"*

9

WHAT ARE ANGEL CARDS?

"Open your mind to listen and your eyes to see,
and let your angels guide you to where you should be"

Mary Jac

Angel cards are a set of cards, each one bearing individual images and messages inspired by angels. There are many different decks of angel cards available to buy. Each deck can vary in size from 25 cards through to hundreds of cards.

Therefore, with so many angel card decks to choose from, you may be wondering *"what is the best deck of Angel cards to use?"*

The answer to this is simple; choose the deck of cards that you feel resonates most powerfully with you. It is important that you like the imagery on the cards you are using and that you feel able to work with them. Some angel card decks will be more appealing to you than others. Choose the ones that have the colours, layout and imagery that you prefer most. As time goes on and you become more practiced and confident in reading the cards, you may wish to add more decks to your collection. This can be very useful as it gives you different ways of reading and interpreting messages. I have found that connecting well with your Angels enables you to read just about any deck of cards and to obtain deep insight, guidance and meaningful messages. It really is that simple.

How do angel cards differ to tarot cards?

Tarot cards were originally used as a card game from the mid 15th century. The symbolism and words on tarot cards made them useful as a method of divination; predicting the future. Some of the imagery and wording on tarot cards can be a little unnerving.

Angel cards however, use very gentle, uplifting and positive images and language. They are easier to understand and interpret than tarot cards. Even if you have never seen a particular deck of Angel cards before, you can pick them up and begin interpreting them very quickly by reading the words on each card, observing the imagery and reading the notes in the accompanying guide book.

The idea behind angel cards is to ask a question and select one or more cards. The images and words on the cards act like direct guidance from your guardian angels.

Here I will show you how to shuffle, draw and interpret messages from any deck of angel cards. These are just some of the ways that reading angel cards can help you in everyday life:

Angel cards:

- enable you to feel a stronger, more direct connection with your Angels
- give you direction and guidance
- give you answers to important questions
- help you find your life purpose
- guide you in making decisions

- can forewarn you about potential events and outcomes of situations

- give you reassurance about any fears and worries

- help reinforce your faith that your angels are always looking after you.

Most of all, angel cards are like having a direct connection with your angels. These little cards provide uplifting messages through words and images of peace, love and hope.

10

PREPARING FOR A READING

*"I wear a coat of angels' breath and warm
myself with their love"*

Emme Woodhull Bache

Before you begin using your angel cards there are some certain steps I would advise you to take to cleanse the cards and the space you are working within. I also strongly advise protecting yourself, because you will be opening your crown chakra to receive guidance.

Clearing and imprinting your energy onto the cards

The cards will have been handled by a lot of other people during the process of printing, collating and transporting them. Now that a particular deck of cards belongs to you, it's a good idea to cleanse them of other people's energy and to imprint them with your own energy.

You may remember me discussing earlier in the book, the concept of the chakras in the palms of your hands. We will be using the energies within these chakras to cleanse the cards and imprint them with energy. I'm going to share with you a practice that Doreen Virtue recommends following when using angel cards for the first time.

Remove your angel cards from their packaging. One by one, touch each of the cards. This is a good way of loosening up the cards to make them easier to shuffle. The coatings on them can make them stick together. It is also a good way to familiarise yourself with the deck and to make the cards familiar with your energy.

Place the cards in the hand you don't write with - this hand receives energy. Hold the hand you write with over the deck - this is the hand that gives energy. Imagine white light leaving the palm of your hand and travelling down through the deck of cards.

As you do, say the following words out loud or in your mind:

"Thank you angels for lifting away anything from these cards that is not divine love."

It is entirely up to you if you would like to allow other people to handle and use your angel cards. If you do, then make sure that you follow this process each time you use the cards again.

Another way of clearing the energy from the cards is to give the deck two or three sharp knocks, just as you would if you were knocking on a door.

If you are reserving your deck of angels cards for your personal use only (and they are stored inside their box or bag in between uses), there is no need to do the clearing every time.

Clearing the space

The space where you are doing your readings will contain the energy from other people who have passed through it. You can also bring energy into your home and personal space from having mixed with people. Cleansing your space regularly is an important process to follow, not just for angel card reading but for your own wellbeing.

If you are reading for other people, then I would highly recommend clearing the space after the reading too.

Here are different space-clearing methods you may wish to try:

- Open the doors and windows to let fresh air circulate and to remove old energies.
- Use sound to remove energy such as clapping your hands or ringing a bell. Walk around when you are doing this and go right into the corners of the room. Stretch your hands up as far as possible and go down to your ankles to ensure all areas are covered.
- Imagine that there is a white light pouring through the ceiling and flooding the whole room, dissolving any negative energy and replacing it with pure, loving energy.
- Burn a scented candle or some incense to clear the space. Certain essential oils and fragrances such as lavender, lemon, peppermint, sage and eucalyptus are excellent for clearing and also for allowing angelic energy to flow more readily.

I am a big fan of using scented candles and always light a candle ten minutes before I do a reading. I continue to burn the candle throughout the reading and blow out the flame only when I have completely finished and packed my cards away.

Protecting yourself before a reading

When you are reading angel cards, to connect more closely with your angels you will either consciously or unconsciously open your crown chakra. This is the energy centre on the top of your head. The crown chakra allows the angels to connect with you most powerfully during a reading and this is the channel their light and energy flows through most readily to give you guidance. To allow only beautiful, divine angelic energy to enter through your crown chakra, it is important to protect yourself. Here are some of the ways in which you can do this.

Forming a protective bubble

Imagine that there is a bubble of light all around you like a force field. Make sure that as you are imagining this bubble, it encapsulates you completely; encircling your whole body. Imagine that the bubble expands so that it contains the total area around you by four feet. Your aura radiates outwards by up to three feet, so you want to ensure that your aura is protected as well as your body. When you come to open your channels for guidance the angelic energy will be able to penetrate the bubble, because that is your intention; nothing else can.

Wearing a virtual cloak

This is a technique I learned from my lovely friend Peta Gelder who is a holistic therapist and a wonderful teacher of all things spiritual (Peta has definitely been one of my fairy godmothers!) She imagines putting on a cloak to protect herself. She even goes so far as to suggest that you should put this cloak on every day after you've bathed/showered, so that you are protected from negative energy wherever you go.

She imagines placing the cloak on and that the fabric of the cloak covers every part of the body including the head; the cloak has a magnificent hood. You may wish your cloak to have very long sleeves so that it covers your fingers or perhaps the sleeves have gloves built into them. To protect your face, you might want to imagine the hood has a transparent veil at the front so that you can still see and connect with people but your face is protected.

Peta has such a fantastic sense of humour and is a great story teller. When she describes the concept of the virtual cloak, she talks of having a whole wardrobe of cloaks. She imagines each of them being in different colours with a multitude of coloured and patterned linings. So she can select a protective cloak depending upon her mood or what she wants to manifest into her life. I love the idea of this!

Saying an angel prayer

Before you begin any angel card reading you may wish to say a prayer. A prayer is basically sending a request out to your angels. In doing so, you are asking them to give you guidance and also to protect you by giving you information that is only for your highest good and for the highest good of the person for whom you are reading.

This is the angel prayer I use and have slightly adapted from the angel prayer recommended by Doreen Virtue. You may wish to use this or to adapt it with words you find more appropriate:

"Dear angels thank you for always strengthening and protecting me and for helping me to tune in to your divine guidance and wisdom.

I am open to receiving any messages you have to offer me and ask that only pure and trustworthy messages come through this reading and the use of these cards. I ask that this card reading bring blessings to all involved."

When you begin doing angel card readings for yourself, remember to have your faithful angel journal by your side, to make notes of the messages within the cards.

I also like to take a photograph of certain spreads with my phone. You can keep it in a photo album on your phone or print it out and paste it into your journal so you can look back at the spread. It is fascinating to see how the advice from the cards manifests and unfolds in our lives.

Alcohol

I would advise against drinking alcohol or taking drugs (legal or otherwise) before doing an angel card reading. Alcohol and drugs can weaken the aura. They also act as either stimulants or depressants and affect our mood and our ability to be intuitive.

11

SELECTING ANGEL CARDS

*"If you can't hear the angels, try quieting
the static of worry"*

Valentine Sterling

Shuffling the cards

Whenever you are ready to begin a reading, the first step is to shuffle the cards so that they are well mixed and you will avoid drawing cards from a previous reading.

Shuffle the cards in any way that you feel most comfortable. When I first started out with tarot cards many years ago, I was taught to deal them into seven equal piles; then collate the card deck together again and shuffle. This is a very good way of ensuring the cards are well distributed, particularly when using your card deck for the very first time.

Shuffle the cards until you feel that they have been shuffled enough. Over time, your intuition will tell you exactly when to stop.

Selecting the cards

After shuffling, there are different ways in which you may wish to select the cards for your angel reading.

Creating a fan

Place the cards down and with your dominant hand (the hand you write with) pull the cards out into a fan shape.

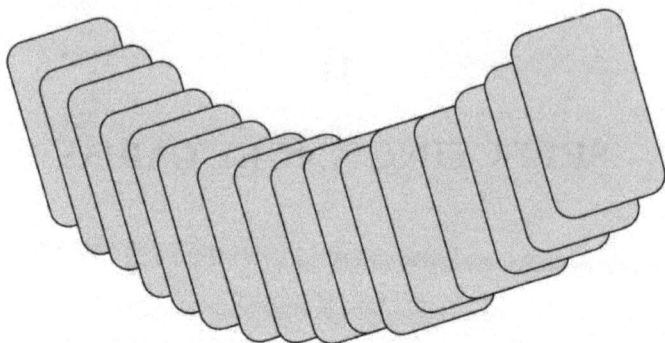

You can then select the cards at random. You may choose to select a certain card because it is sticking out more than the others. You can also hover over the cards with your non-dominant hand (the hand you don't write with) to sense or feel which cards should be selected.

Dealing from the top of the deck

After shuffling, you may feel that you wish to select the cards by taking them one, by one from the top of the deck. My daughter prefers to select cards using this method. She also takes a look at the card that is at the bottom of the deck, to see what influences it has on the reading.

Selecting cards as you shuffle

This is the method of card selection I prefer to use. I shuffle the cards a few times and then as I continue shuffling, certain cards push themselves upwards out of the deck and I select those. If you use this method be mindful that on certain occasions you will try to pull out a certain card and it feels as though it is stuck or doesn't come out easily. This is a message to you that the card wasn't meant to be selected, so keep on shuffling.

Jumping cards

When you are shuffling, a card sometimes jumps out of the deck or you drop an individual card in the process of shuffling. These cards are known as 'jumpers'. It is up to you whether you wish to place any significance on a 'jumper'. Whether you choose to use the card as part of your reading or not, it is well worth taking a look at the card to see what the message is.

Many times I have had a card jump out and then I have put it back in the deck. When I am drawing cards this card has come out again. So do pay attention to the jumpers, because they often have something important to tell us.

People often ask me about choosing the right cards. They wonder if they have made the wrong choice and in that case, how will this affect the reading? My response to this is that you can never choose the wrong cards.

Your angels are guiding you and you are following your intuition in the shuffling and selecting of the cards, so just trust that it is right. The other important thing to consider here is that the interpreting of the cards is the most important thing; not the cards themselves.

What I mean by this is, you can draw the same card for two different people and it will signify different things. What is most important within angel card reading is delving into your intuition and saying what you see and what comes into your mind. Believe me, as your angel card reading skills and your angelic connections develop, you will see more and more messages within the cards.

12

ANGEL CARD SPREADS

*"Let your Angelic light shine and guide
others who need the light to find themselves"*

Sue K

Angel cards can be used for guidance as much or little as you like. You may wish to draw a card every day at a certain time to ask for some support and advice from your angels. You can use the cards to gain wisdom and insight into particular questions or to ask about different life circumstances. The number of cards you select and the meaning you attach to their placement is known as a spread. In this chapter I would like to share with you some of my favourite spreads and how they can be a very valuable way of channelling messages and guidance from your angels.

One card

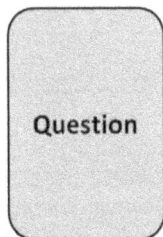

One-card readings can be very powerful. I find that selecting one card is very good for:

- answering a specific question i.e. **"what will be the outcome of this situation?"**
- daily guidance from your guardian angel
- answering direct question with a 'yes' or 'no'

When you are selecting this one card, ask the question out loud or hold the question in your mind you would like the answer to or guidance around.

Two cards

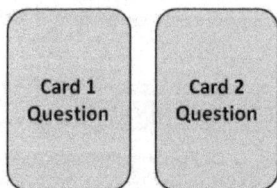

Use two cards whenever you want to uncover more information about a certain question.

So for example, your main question with card number 1 might be: *"What does the day/week/month ahead hold for me?"*

Card number 2 can be used to further illustrate this by asking:

"What is your advice to me?" or

"How can I be most effective this day/week/month?"

Three cards

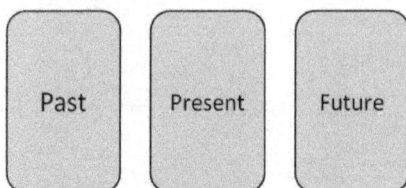

The three card reading is an excellent way of asking about the past, present and future of a situation. When you are doing an angel reading for yourself, you don't need to know about the past so you could use just two cards if you wish. However, I do like to use three cards because it is a good confirmation for me that I have chosen the right cards and that I am connected when I see the card that relates to the past is very meaningful to me.

The time frame of each of these cards is entirely up to you. Be specific when asking your angels and drawing the cards. Typically, I ask for the past to relate to the past six months. The present to relate to right now and the coming six weeks; I call this 'the just over the horizon card'. The future relates to the next six months.

When you are starting out doing readings for yourself and other people, this spread is so simple and yet gives so much information. If you want to keep a reading very short and sweet but also give plenty of insight to someone, then this is the perfect spread.

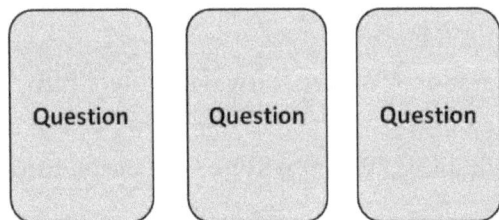

Question	Question	Question

What I particularly like to do, to extend and validate the three card spread, is to draw three cards from two different angel card decks (six cards in total). It is amazing of the cards will be similar in meaning even though you have taken them from different card decks. That gives even more confirmation that you have connected well with your angels.

You can also use the three-card spread to gain deeper insight into a particular issue, such as career, finances, love, life path, etc. As you select each card, think of a question you would like the answer to. For example if you had a question about your career:

1. Card number 1 question might be: **"What is the right career for me?"**
2. Card number 2 question might be: **"How can I get onto this career path?"**
3. Card number 3 question might be: **"What should my next step be?"**

The three-card spread is particularly good for a reading for the month. Card number one signifies the beginning of the month; card number two is the middle of the month and card number three is the end of the month.

Here is how I like to use the three-card spread for love and romance readings:

1. Card number 1 question: **"Who is the person who is right for me?"**
2. Card number 2 question: **"Where/how will I meet him/her?"**
3. Card number 3 question: **"When will he/she come into my life?"**

My daughter calls this the **"Who is (s)he; where is (s)he; when is (s)he coming"** reading!

Nine cards

The nine-card spread is an extension of the three-card spread, and can give an interesting insight into a variety of different areas of your own and other people's lives. Here is what the different cards signify.

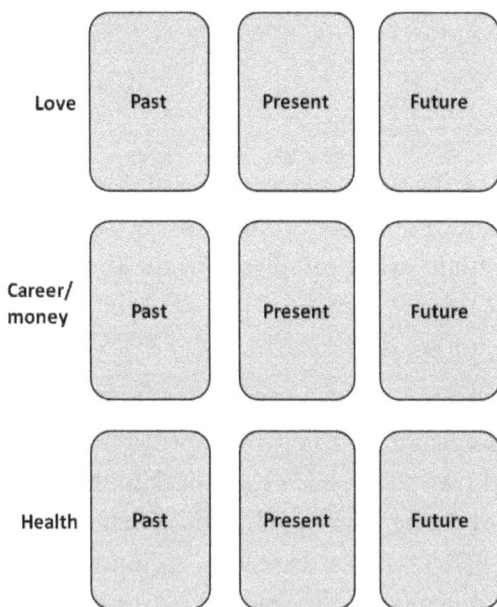

	Past	Present	Future
Love	Past	Present	Future
Career/ money	Past	Present	Future
Health	Past	Present	Future

This spread is very simple, but it gives a lot of detail to you or the person you a reading for. These three areas are typically the main things that people want guidance and support around. I also find that it is far easier to concentrate on just three rows of cards that relate to three key areas. If you do a reading using more than nine cards it can get very confusing trying to remember the significance of each different card.

I have given examples of the meanings that each card row could be connected to. You can substitute these for any area of life that you wish. For example, you might want to place money and career as two separate rows. People often like to ask about life purpose, spirituality, learning, home and family.

You can do this reading with one deck of angel cards. If you acquire more decks of cards you might want to use a different deck for each row. For example, I often use the 'Romance Angel Card Deck' for the love section. I might use the 'Archangel Power Tarot' for career and money and the 'Flower Therapy' cards for health.

The Celtic Cross

This spread is a one of the most widely used spreads in tarot and oracle card reading. It consists of 10 cards. Six cards are placed selected in a certain order and placed in the shape of a cross. A further four cards are drawn and placed to the right of the cross in a column known as the staff.

When I first began working with oracle cards when I was sixteen years old, I really didn't like the Celtic Cross spread. I found it hard to remember and very confusing. I came back to the Celtic Cross when I began working with angel cards. What I found most confusing was that certain cards seemed to repeat themselves or have no relevance upon the reading. I constantly had to refer to a book when I was doing a reading, so I decided to attach my own meaning to the placements of each card; meaning that you could recall much more easily. I find this works wonderfully for me now. If you ever have a reading with me, this is the spread I will always lay out first. It gives me a broad picture of where you have come from and where you are heading, what advice your angels have for you, your strengths, your challenges, the people surrounding you and the outcome over the next 12 months.

The Celtic Cross is a very powerful spread because it gives you a complete picture of the person you are reading for; whether that is you or someone else. The cards are all interconnected and important themes begin to emerge from the reading. It is also a reading where quite a few different aspects of life can come up, so it is a spread that is worth persevering with.

Here is my own version of the Celtic Cross. The instruction booklet within many of the angel card decks contains the traditional version of the Celtic Cross, so I would advise you to try both my version and the traditional one to see which you prefer. You may also wish to adapt this spread and make it your own. In my version of the Celtic Cross shown I place the cards in a slightly different sequence.

Important factors to consider within the Celtic Cross

When you are reading the messages within the Celtic Cross it is important that you look at how the cards are connected to one another. You can turn each card over one at a time and read each one individually or you can turn all the cards over at once.

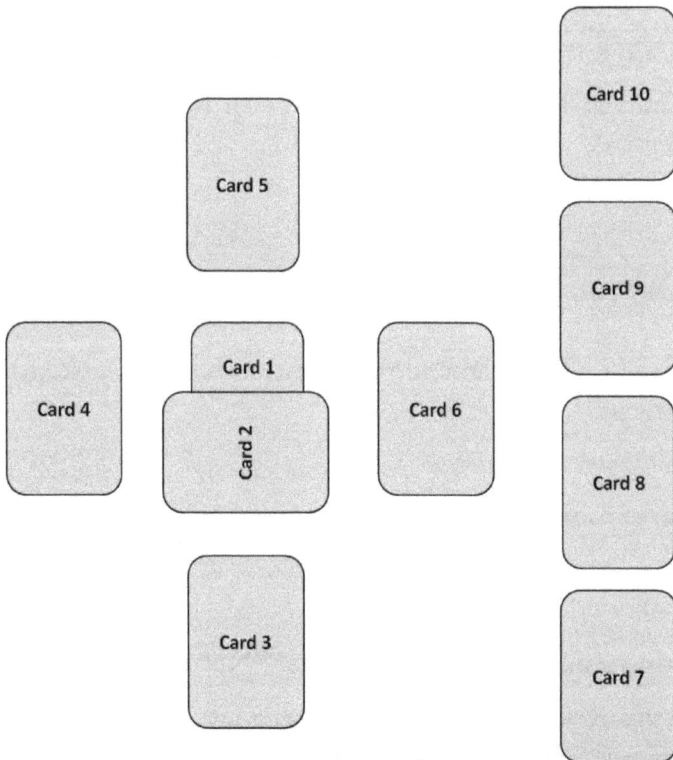

Card 10

Card 5

Card 9

Card 1

Card 4   Card 2   Card 6

Card 8

Card 3

Card 7

Card 1: The present time. What is going on right now?

Card 2: The challenge. What is affecting the current situation? Even a positive card drawn here can be challenging

Card 3: The basis of the situation. What is in your subconscious mind?

Card 4: The past. What has happened over the last 6 to 12 months that has impacted on today

Card 5: The horizon. What is coming up over the next 6 to 8 weeks?

Card 6: The near future. What is coming up over the next 6 months?

Card 7: Your strength in the situation

Card 8: The advice. What your angels want you to know

Card 9: The people around you and their thoughts and feelings

Card 10: The outcome. Where will you be 12 months from now?

Be sure to glance around the spread to see what patterns are emerging.

What colours do you see?

What archangels/animals/elements are particularly prevalent?

Where are these aspects clustered in relation to the past, present and future?

Asking a question with a "Yes" or "No" answer

For this type of spread I favour using just one card. Drawing more than one card can get very confusing.

Shuffle the card and hold the question in your mind that you would like an answer to. Use your instincts to know when you have shuffled for long enough and which card to draw.

Some angel cards decks are designed to give direct, yes or no answers to questions. In this case you will be given an answer that is easy to interpret. If you are using a more general deck of angel cards then look at the card you have drawn.

Yes

Is the message on the card very positive, happy, joyful or magical? This would signify a "Yes" answer.

No

Is it advising caution, patience, further consideration, solitude, sadness, or letting go of a situation? This would signify a "No" to your question.

If you are in any doubt then shuffle again and draw a second card. If this leaves you in doubt once more, your angels are telling you that the situation is undecided or it is not in your best interests to know the answer right now.

Timing of events

We often want to know when certain things in our lives will happen. Here is a technique that I learned during my workshop with Doreen Virtue and Radleigh Valentine. It is a very good way of getting an indication of timing.

Shuffle the angel card deck and ask the question in your mind *"when will this happen?"*

When your intuition tells you, stop shuffling then select a card. If the card has a number on it, this signifies the number of weeks, months or years within which the event will take place. Shuffle again to ask "Is this weeks?" then draw another card.

Use "Yes" or "No" technique to ascertain whether your angels are telling you it will happen within weeks. If the answer is yes, you can stop there. If the answer is no, then shuffle again and draw another card to ask whether this will happen within months. If the answer is still no, then repeat the process to ask about years.

You can also use your intuition to ask yourself, does this card number signify weeks, months of years? Whatever feels right to you is the answer.

I hope you find my suggested spreads useful. Don't be afraid to adapt these, experiment and be creative with trying out your own spreads. You will find that the more practice you have with angel cards, the more your intuition will guide you to try out your own methods.

13

INTERPRETING ANGEL CARDS

*"If one looks closely enough, one can
see angels in every piece of art"*

Adeline Cullen Ray

When you first begin reading angel cards you are learning, it is all new, so you will be working mostly with your logical mind. This is an excellent place to start.

It is important not to rush the process of tapping into your intuition; this will happen in its own good time. One thing I can assure you of is this; it will happen for you.

Words

The very biggest advantage of angel cards is that they contain words. When you first begin reading angel cards, your eyes will automatically be drawn to the title of the card and the words that describe the meaning of it. I would definitely advise you to read the words and to look at the guide book that accompanies those cards. This will help you become acquainted with the meanings of your cards.

It is also worth writing notes in your angel journal about the cards you have drawn.

Which words stood out for you?

When you saw a particular word, what significance did this have?

This recording of notes and questioning enables you to connect with your higher self. Before long you will be doing this as second nature and instead of reaching for the guide book, you will be making your own interpretations.

Practice makes perfect; the more readings you do, the more familiar you will become with your card deck.

Colours

Colours within the cards have very important messages to bear. When you look at a single angel card, the colours will be the first things that are obvious to you. Colours carry different meanings and messages, so I'd like to share with you some of the research I have done, to help you apply meaning to the different angel cards you select within your readings.

COLOUR	MEANING
White	The colour of purity. Our quest for perfection and balance; enabling us to see all sides of a situation. White reflects colours and mirrors who we are back at us. White is also the colour of divinely-guided inspiration. The light of our guardian angels. Associated with the element of Air and Water.
Violet/ purple	This colour is about our self-worth, our integrity, focus and dedication to a cause or a piece of work. It is the colour of spirituality and transformation. Inspiration; vision; life purpose. It is also the colour that represents the crown chakra. Associated with the element of Fire.

Blue	Represents power and masculine energy; positive thinking Communication; honesty; trust; peace; loyally. Blue represents the throat chakra. The light of Archangel Michael. Associated with the element of Air and water.
Green	Harmony; healing; New beginnings; love. Compassion; home and family. Comfort; positive change. The colour of the heart chakra. The light of Archangel Raphael. Associated with the elements of Earth and Water.
Yellow	Inner peace; bliss; confidence; creativity. Happiness; sunshine; hope. Shining your light in the world. Self awareness and broadmindedness. Can also indicate travel. The colour of the solar plexus chakra. Associated with the elements of Fire and Earth.
Gold	Inner knowing; wisdom; following and embracing your bliss. Seeing the light; spiritual abundance. Protection and cleansing. The light of Archangel Gabriel. Associated with the element of Fire.
Orange	Spontaneity; enthusiasm; fun; laughter and a sense of humour. Lightness of being. Playfulness and being yourself. Good health and vitality. The colour of the sacral chakra. Associated with the elements of Fire and Earth.

Red	The colour of courage, passion and survival. A surge of energy and strength; taking the initiative. Change and movement. Growth, action and forward motion. It can also denote anger; a strong force of will and control. Reaching an important goal. The colour of the base chakra. Associated with the element of Fire.
Pink	Represents feminine energy; unconditional love; abundance. This colour can indicate sensitivity; comfort; following one's heart. Going with the flow. Associated with the elements of Earth and Water.
Brown	Material possessions; money; land; our home. Hard work; the harvest; strong friendships with like-minded people. The outdoors; the healing power of nature. Associated with the element of Earth.
Grey	Stretching oneself; new ideas; persevering towards a goal. Fulfilling long-awaited ambitions. Being a gifted communicator; mind over matter. Associated with the element of Air.
Black	Black signifies surrendering and letting go. Life's mysteries; going within; solitude. The darkest hour before the dawn. The beginning of a whole new life chapter. Associated with the element of Water.

Imagery

The thing that I love most about angel cards is their beautiful imagery. Unlike tarot cards, every single angel card is positive and uplifting. Some cards have much more rich and complex imagery than others. When you are starting out with angel cards it's a good idea to work with cards that have a lot of detail in the pictures. This will help you to channel angelic messages much more effectively just by looking at the picture and seeing what stands out to you.

I have included an image from one of my own deck of cards, the 'by Natalia Angel Oracle Deck'.

Take a careful look at the card and write some notes about it.

When you look at this card, what do you see?

What else do you notice?

What is the theme of this card?

What is this card saying to you?

What does this mean?

Congratulations! You have just read and interpreted the messages within an angel card. I deliberately left out the wording on the card so that you could concentrate on the imagery.

So when you draw any angel card, you can interpret a general message from the angels or you can apply the meaning to whatever question or subject you would like to focus upon.

Now let's consider: what would the meaning of this card be if it was drawn in relation to a question about:

- Love?
- *Money?*
- *Career?*
- *Life purpose?*
- *Home/family?*
- *Health?*
- *Spirituality?*

Here is my interpretation of this card. Remember there is no and right and wrong with angel card reading. Whatever messages you pick up or conclusions you come to are exactly right for you.

Card title: Balance and healing

Card description:

Getting your life back into balance

Healing from physical ailments

Acceptance of yourself and who you are

"This card is all about experiencing the miracle of being in balance. Balance can sometimes feel strange to us because we are so often out of balance. We experience life's highs when we are feeling on top of the world and at our peak. We also experience the lows, when things do not turn out how we would like them to, we feel sad, lonely, disillusioned or depressed. Balance is the perfect place in the middle. The calm place, where nothing is good or bad; it simply is. We are in harmony with everything and everyone around us. Our energy levels are balanced and we are able to flow along with life.

Being in balance is like the holy grail of human existence. It is about accepting that where we are is exactly where we need to be at this point in time. The lady in this picture is holding her arms aloft to ensure she maintains her balance. The sphere she is standing upon could tip her off and send her flying either upwards or downwards, so she has had to learn how to get into this position and how to maintain it. She has learned what works for her and what does not. This is the key to life, hence the image of the keyhole.

The images of flowers beneath her skirt; the leaves to the right of her and the flower petals on the sphere signify her blossoming to reach this place; this state of balance and serenity."

Let's do another exercise with a second card.

Powerful Connections

TWIN Flame

Meeting of two like-minded souls
An important love relationship
Unity & balance in partnerships

When you look at this card, what do you see?

What else do you notice?

What is the theme of this card?

What is this card saying to you?

What does this mean?

This is my own interpretation of the card. How does it compare to yours?

Card title: Powerful connections

Card description:

A meeting of two like-minded souls

An important love relationship

Unity & balance in partnerships

"This card shows the union between two souls. They are in such perfect harmony with one another as their movements are synchronised. They fit together effortlessly and are strongly connected. One is not happier than the other, they are both overjoyed in equal measure and they are completely lost in the moment. If you are single and would like to invite love into your life, this card is a reminder to have faith that there is someone who will be a perfect fit for you. It feels as though the full moon will play a big part in this. At the full moon, write down a list of the qualities you are looking for in a love partner. At the full moon, do a meditation with Archangel Raphael to ask him to help bring your soul mate to you. If you have just met someone new, the chances are that this is 'the one' there will certainly be sparks flying!

So let's consider. What would the meaning of this card be if it was drawn in relation to a question about:

- Love?
- *Money?*
- *Career?*
- *Life purpose?*
- *Home/family?*
- *Health?*
- *Spirituality?*

If you are in an existing relationship, this is an important time to connect with your loved one at a deeper level. The full moon is a significant time for strengthening your loving bond, so watch out for this time period. Make an extra special effort to be together and to share open and loving communication."

Reading intuitively

Your intuition is always there, it doesn't change but during the course of meditating, connecting with your angels and reading angel cards, you will become much more mindful of it. In the same way that when we are looking at buying a certain car, we suddenly see the type of car everywhere; our awareness becomes engaged with it. Doing this angel work really heightens your ability to tune in to your intuition much more powerfully.

So you will find that when you are doing angel card readings, words, images and ideas pop into your head seemingly from nowhere. There is no need to be alarmed, this is your angels connecting to you through your intuition and it is a wonderful thing.

This angelic intuition feeds, guides and supports you as you connect with the messages within the cards to build a broader and more detailed picture.

When you are reading angel cards your intuition will serve you very well with interpreting the messages within them. Just say whatever you see, feel, sense, intuit. Don't feel silly about it. As Doreen Virtue says, *"just blurt it out!"*

I have so many example of this from my own experience and this one stands out in particular.

When I was giving a reading to a lady in China over Skype I drew a particular angel card. We were discussing what would be happening for her at Christmas time and for some reason I got an image in my mind of her walking around in Paris. I knew this lady lived in China, I couldn't imagine why I was thinking of Paris, yet I still told her what I had seen this lady was delighted. She told me she had a property in Paris and had been hoping she could spend Christmas there.

No matter how far fetched your intuitive thoughts and ideas are, say them and write them down in your angel journal. Something that seems crazy and completely left of field might have huge significance further down the line.

Above all else; remember to trust your intuition and never feel afraid of following it.

Closing and grounding yourself

After doing meditation and angel card readings it is important to close your crown chakra and ground yourself. Connecting with the angelic energy and with your higher self can leave you light headed. Closing and grounding is an important final step.

Closing your crown chakra

Close your eyes and imagine your crown chakra being like a flower. Imagine the petals of this flower closing up tightly. Say in your mind or out loud

"Thank you angels for your wisdom, guidance and support."

Grounding

Eat a piece of chocolate, a banana or a piece of bread, or drink a cup of tea or coffee. Choose something that will be filling. In doing so, this ensures that we are connected with earthly things once more.

14

ANGELIC CRYSTALS AND MANIFESTING

Angelic crystals

I first began working with gemstones crystals when I took up jewellery making as an off-shoot of my fashion styling work. I have worked for several years with gemstones crystals and little by little I discovered the healing, strengthening and protective properties of these stones

There are so many varieties of crystals in the world; too many to go into detail about here. A lot of books have been written on this subject. If this is something that interests you, take a look at the Directory at the end of this book for some ideas about further resources.

Here I will share with you some of the crystals that will help you develop your angelic connections and will also help to strengthen your aura, lift your mood and manifest what you want into your life.

Recommended Use

Crystal	Angelic Connection	Luck	Love	Money	Career	Protection	Health/Healing	Spirituality/Intuition
Agate							✓	
Alexandrite	✓				✓			✓
Amazonite		✓	✓				✓	
Amethyst	✓	✓	✓			✓	✓	✓
Ametrine	✓			✓		✓	✓	✓
Angelite	✓	✓	✓		✓	✓	✓	✓
Aquamarine			✓				✓	
Bloodstone							✓	
Carnelian							✓	
Chrysoberyl					✓			
Citrine	✓	✓		✓	✓		✓	✓
Danburite	✓	✓	✓				✓	✓
Druzy	✓	✓					✓	✓

Recommended Use

Crystal	Angelic Connection	Luck	Love	Money	Career	Protection	Health/ Healing	Spirituality/ Intuition
Emerald	✓	✓	✓				✓	✓
Fire opal				✓		✓	✓	✓
Fluorite	✓							✓
Garnet		✓		✓			✓	
Haematite	✓	✓	✓				✓	
Iolite	✓							✓
Jade	✓	✓					✓	
Jasper		✓					✓	
Kunzite	✓		✓				✓	
Lepidolite		✓	✓			✓		
Malachite				✓				
Moonstone	✓		✓		✓		✓	✓
Prehnite	✓		✓					✓

Recommended Use

Crystal	Angelic Connection	Luck	Love	Money	Career	Protection	Health/Healing	Spirituality/Intuition
Quartz (blue)	✓		✓			✓		
Quartz (clear)	✓							✓
Quartz (rose)			✓				✓	
Quartz (smokey)		✓		✓				
Rhodonite			✓				✓	
Sapphire	✓			✓	✓			
Tiger's eye		✓	✓			✓	✓	
Topaz (imperial)			✓	✓			✓	
Turquoise		✓	✓			✓	✓	

Purifying and cleansing crystals

Crystals are very energetic and absorb vibrations and negative energy just as easily as they absorb positive energy. Whether you have just bought your crystals, already own them or they were given to you; they need to be cleansed and purified. Here are some different methods you can use.

i. Salt-water purification

One of the best ways of cleansing and purifying a crystal is to place it in distilled water mixed with sea salt. Place half a litre of water in a bowl along with half a teaspoon of sea salt. Allow the salt to dissolve and then place your crystals inside the salt water. Leave them to purify for 24 hours. After 24 hours, rinse the stones in purified water (unsalted).

Avoid placing angelite in salt water because it is a very soft stone and was formed without water. Wetting angelite for long periods can change the properties of the stone.

ii. Crystal clustering

Take a large, light coloured crystal, such as a piece of clear quartz and place it in direct sunlight for a few hours (or moonlight if the moon is full). Bring your large crystal back inside and place the smaller crystals next to it so that that they can be cleansed and purified by the larger stone.

iii.   Smudging

Pass your crystals through the smoke of scented incense such as frankincense or sage.

Manifesting with a crystal grid

Crystals are an excellent way of helping you to set an intention and manifest things that you would like to come into your life.

A crystal grid is a placement of crystals in a geometric pattern. The placement of the crystals directs the energy towards a goal. The number of stones that are used and the fact that they are all leading towards the central goal, amplifies the energy and becomes a powerful way of manifesting your intentions.

1. Set your intention

Decide very clearly what you want your angels to help you manifest. Take a small piece of paper and write your intention on it in the present tense and with gratitude. For example:

"Thank you angels for bringing me…"

2. Cleanse the crystal grid location

Decide where you would like you crystal grid to be. Choose a place out of the way where the grid will not be disturbed. Cleanse the space by burning a candle or some incense or a sage stick. Refer back to chapter 10 for further information about space clearing. Place a cloth on the table or work surface where you will be setting up the grid.

3. Visualise

Fold up the piece of paper that has your intention written on it. Place it in the centre of the crystal grid cloth. Breathe in deeply through your nose and inflate your belly as you breathe in. Hold your breath for a few seconds and exhale through your nose. Repeat this seven times and as you breathe in and out, visualise your intention in your mind.

4. Place and activate the crystals

Place a large crystal in the centre of the grid on top of the folded paper. Position the other crystals in the grid according to the particular geometric shaped grid you are creating. Take a pointed quartz and starting from the outside work in a clockwise direction. Draw an invisible line with the quartz point to 'energetically' connect each crystal to the next. This is just like 'connecting the dots'.

5. **Timescales**

Your grid is now activated. Leave your crystal grid in place for around 40 days. You can burn some candles around it if you wish. You can also position next to it any angel cards that relate to your intentions or an angel ornament.

Here are two grid shapes for different intentions. You can use different shapes and sizes of stones.

A general grid

Use at least two different types of crystals that correspond with the intention you would like to manifest. For example, use rose quartz and amazonite for love.

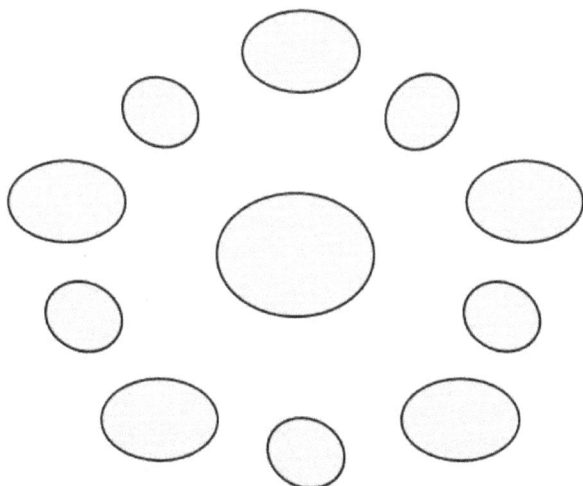

A grid for money/career

The crystals are arranged in the shape of the infinity symbol to bring endless abundance with career and money. Use the stones that correspond with your specific intention.

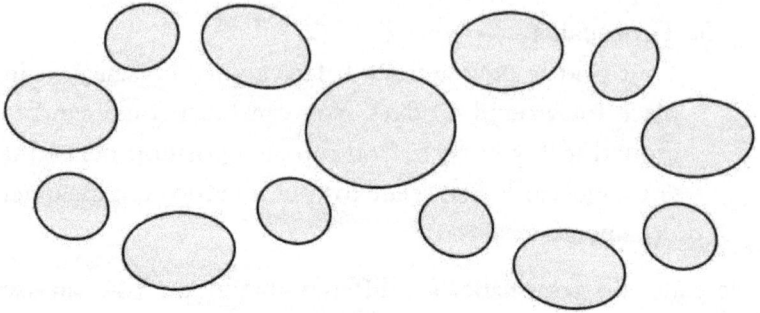

AFTERWORD

"Brighter and more beautiful than any star,
even in the darkness you sparkle,
your laughter warms like sunshine,
sweet and more comforting than chocolate,
you are pure loveliness"

By Natalia Colman

I hope you have enjoyed going on this angel wisdom journey with me. My life has been a very interesting experience and certainly much more colourful, bright and beautiful since I discovered how to connect with the angels.

So where am I now? Well, I know I am not perfect and I accept myself just as I am. I'm not fixed because I was never broken in the first place. I was tested, put under pressure and my responses to all those tests were dominated by fear. I now see myself as complete. What I mean by this is I feel that I have everything I need within myself. I am not searching for anything else to make me feel better or to fill a void. I have filled the void that I felt in earlier life with love; love for myself and love for those around me.

I no longer blame the people who I encountered on my life's path, I have compassion for them and I forgive them. I do not feel lonely any more because I see the connection between me and everyone else. We are all going along our path in life, accepting the tests that we have chosen and trying to deal with them in the best way we can. That is the connection. We are all different and no one person is better than another. We all look different, we have all had different upbringings, and we have been given different personality types, skills and abilities. What we have been given does not make us better or worse than anybody else; it makes us unique. Everyone has fears and everyone wants to love and be loved, that is the connection between us. We all have a guardian angel who loves us because we are all lovable and worthy of love.

My intention for this book is to share the things I have learned, and to help as many people as I can by telling my story. If this book helps just one person heal in some way, find their inner calm centre, release fear or recognise a part of themselves within my experiences, then it will have been worth writing. I want to help you forgive yourself for anything you have done in the past that still troubles you.

Forgiveness sounds so simple but it is often the most difficult thing to do. You may be surprised to learn that two years ago when I began the process of falling back in love with myself I faced my fears and called Daniel. I called him from a different number because I assumed he would not answer if he knew it was me. When he answered the phone I gently said *"Hello this is Natalia"* he took a sharp intake of breath and immediately spat back at me *"What the hell do you want?"* I spoke very softly and deliberately *"I know you must be surprised to hear from me. I don't want anything from you but all I would like for you to listen for one minute; I have something I really need to tell you."* He fell silent at the other end of the phone and I continued speaking *"I want to have this final conversation with you to release any bad feeling between us. I feel as though there is still a connection, but not a good one because it is based on all the things that happened when we broke up.*

I want to tell you that I forgive everything that happened between us and I wish you well and send you love." Daniel immediately broke down in tears at the other end of the phone. He softly whispered *"Thank you."*

That day was a turning point for me. I was terrified about doing it but it felt like absolutely the right thing. I didn't do this for Daniel. I did it for me. Releasing him gave me the momentum I needed to move forward, to clear away the negativity and the connection that we still had between us. Even if you dislike someone, the very fact that you are holding onto the dislike and bad feelings means you are connected. The only time you can break free from that is through forgiveness and love.

Writing this book has been a very healing experience for me. To put into words so many of the things that have happened to me. To see the journey I have been on and where I have arrived today makes me feel truly blessed. I am proud to say that as I finish writing this book, I am just about to go off for lunch with my daughter, my ex-husband and my Dad. Healing my relationship with these two men, who have played such a huge part in my life, has not been easy, but it has been very worthwhile. I forgive what happened between us and I thank them for everything they have taught me.

Most of all I love them and I know that they love me.

I use the word love a lot throughout this book and that is because divine love and human love is the thing that connects us all. Love is my favourite word and it is my favourite thing to do.

Thank you for reading this book and for being part of my continued journey. I wish you a life that is fulfilling and one that is a source of great joy to you. I also wish that you may appreciate your own inner beauty and how magical your life is. May you be truly mindful of this magic every day.

Lots of love and angel blessings to you.

Natalia

DIRECTORY

Here is a list of gurus and resources that I have been inspired by throughout my journey with the angels.

Angel Card Decks

These are my favourite angel card decks:

Angel Answers Oracle Cards (Doreen Virtue)

Archangel Power Tarot Cards (Doreen Virtue and Radleigh Valentine)

Angel of Light Cards (Diana Cooper)

Angel Prayers Oracle Cards (Kyle Gray)

Angel Tarot Cards (Doreen Virtue and Radleigh Valentine)

By Natalia Angel Wisdom Cards (created by me!)

By Natalia Power Word Cards (created by me!)

Daily Guidance From Your Angels Oracle Cards (Doreen Virtue)

Goddess Guidance Oracle Cards (Doreen Virtue)

Flower Therapy Oracle Cards (Doreen Virtue and Robert Reeves)

The Romance Angel Oracle Cards (Doreen Virtue)

Angel Intuitives

Diana Cooper

Diana's angel card deck was the first one I ever purchased. She has worked with angels for many years and is the author of several books and angel card decks.

www.dianacooper.com

Kyle Gray

Kyle is an angel expert, author and motivational speaker. He has written books about angels and speaks at events all over the world and on his YouTube channel about his experiences with the angelic realm. His 'Angel Prayers' card deck is one of my favourite angel card decks with its powerful with very modern imagery.

www.kylegray.co.uk

Doreen Virtue

The original 'Angel Lady' and a huge inspiration to millions of people all over the world through her work with angels. Doreen has written many books and has developed an extensive range of angel card decks.

www.angeltherapy.com

Nicky Williams

An angel practitioner and spiritual healer based in Surrey, UK. Nicky practices the 'Journey Therapy' and has a wonderful process for helping remove emotional blocks. I highly recommend taking a session with her either face to face or via Skype.

www.page2of1.co.uk

Books about crystals

The Crystal Bible
Judy Hall

The Crystal Healing Bible
Sue Lily

Crystal Prescriptions
Judy Hall

Gurus

Mark Abadi

A holistic psychologist, international spiritual teacher and author of the book 'Evolve'. I can highly recommend his book as a guide to finding balance and self acceptance. It's the closest thing to actually having a session with him.

www.syntonium.com

Astrolada

Lada Duncheva is a phenomenal lady who has an 'other-worldly' ability to amass knowledge about all things astrological and eso-teric. She is so generous in sharing her knowledge and observa-tions with the world and is a true inspiration.

www.Astrolada.com

Louise L. Hay

Found of Hay House Publishing and author of the book 'You Can Heal Your Life'. Louise's book did indeed help me heal my life. I have read her book over and over again and I still pick it up and see new messages within it.

www.louisehay.com

Robert Holden

Robert is author of the fabulous book 'Love-ability' and many other uplifting books. He is also a host on Hay House Radio and pioneer of 'The Happiness Project'.

www.robertholden.org

Jack Kornfield

This gentleman was talking about mindfulness long before it was fashionable. His book 'The Wise Heart' was the first book I read on my journey towards transformation all those years ago.

It is a beautiful piece of writing and carries so many wise messages about love, compassion, spiritual and emotional healing.
www.jackkornfield.com

Julie Starr

A coaching expert and best-selling author of a range of coaching and mentoring books. Julie is also an excellent non-fiction writer. Her young–adult novel 'Magic to Memphis' is a gripping story combined with some very thought provoking messages about the meaning of life. She is also a very enlightened being and a great mentor.
www.starrconsulting.co.uk
www.ruffdogbooks.com

Pisces Moon Goddess

This USA-based lady named April, combines deep intuition with a fascination for astrology. Don't be surprised when you see and hear a lot more about this lady in the future. She is a rising star in the world of astrology. Her birth chart reading and predictions for me were so accurate it was uncanny.

Watch her YouTube channel: **piscesmoongoddess**

Steve Taylor

A senior lecturer in psychology at Leeds Beckett University and the author of many best-selling books.

Steve often runs webinars and face-to-face workshops about mindfulness and finding your calm centre.
www.stevenmtaylor.com

Whats-your-sign.com

A website filled with information about spiritual signs and the symbolic meaning of animals, birds and other creatures.
www.whats-your-sign.com

Marianne Williamson

World-renowned author of the very powerful book 'A Course in Miracles'. I can highly recommend her latest book 'A Year of Miracles'. It is meant to be read one chapter at a time, every day. I gave myself this as a gift for my birthday and have found it very uplifting and the messages so appropriate.

www.marianne.com

ABOUT THE AUTHOR

Natalia Colman is a UK-based author, teacher and jewellery designer who loves everything about angels.

Natalia dispenses her wisdom about all things angelic and her monthly angel card readings for the star signs, through www.astrolada.com and on her own YouTube channel: Angels by Natalia

For more information about Natalia's on-line version of 'The Complete Angel Wisdom Workshop' and her other products, news and events, please contact:

www.angelsbynatalia.co.uk
www.facebook.com/angelcardlady
YouTube: Angels by Natalia